The University of Texas at Austin

THE CAMPUS GUIDE

The University of Texas at Austin

AN ARCHITECTURAL TOUR BY

Lawrence W. Speck
and
Richard L. Cleary

WITH PHOTOGRAPHS BY
Casey Dunn

PRINCETON ARCHITECTURAL PRESS
NEW YORK

Published by
Princeton Architectural Press
37 East Seventh Street
New York, New York 10003

For a free catalog of books, call 1.800.722.6657.
Visit our website at www.papress.com.

Series Editor: Nancy Eklund Later
Editor: Dan Simon
Designer: Bree Anne Apperley
Mapmaker: Matt Knutzen

Special thanks to: Sara Bader, Nicola Bednarek Brower,
Janet Behning, Fannie Bushin, Carina Cha, Tom Cho,
Penny (Yuen Pik) Chu, Russell Fernandez, Jan Haux,
Linda Lee, John Myers, Katharine Myers, Margaret Rogalski,
Andrew Stepanian, Jennifer Thompson, Paul Wagner,
Joseph Weston, and Deb Wood of Princeton Architectural Press
—Kevin C. Lippert, publisher

Library of Congress Cataloging-in-Publication Data
Speck, Lawrence W., 1949–
The University of Texas at Austin / architectural tour by Lawrence W.
Speck and Richard L. Cleary; with photographs by Casey Dunn.
     p. cm. — (The campus guide)
Includes bibliographical references and index.
ISBN 978-1-56898-854-2 (alk. paper)
1. University of Texas at Austin—Buildings—Guidebooks. 2. University
of Texas at Austin—Buildings—Pictorial works. 3. Rice University—
Pictorial works. 1. Cleary, Richard 1. 11. Title.
LD5333.S67 2011
378.764'31—dc22

                                                    2010041649

CONTENTS

This book offers an insider's guide to architecture and planning on the main campus of The University of Texas at Austin, from Cass Gilbert's character-defining Battle Hall library building (1910), to Paul Cret's master development plan and ensemble of buildings (1930s), Gordon Bunshaft's Lyndon Baines Johnson Library and Museum (1971), and to Kallman, McKinnell and Wood's Blanton Museum of Art (2003).

The guide opens with an introduction that discusses the historical context of the expansion of the campus from its initial forty acres and the visions of the architects and administrators who created its buildings. The architectural tour consists of six walks examining 107 buildings. The first four walks cover the compact core of the campus while Walks Five and Six range across the more expansive areas to the east and south. Each building is illustrated and discussed with particular attention to its setting, history, and contribution to campus identity. A three-dimensional map accompanies each walk facilitating identification of the buildings.

Visitors are welcome to tour the main campus of The University of Texas at Austin:

Information about the university's orientation centers for visitors and prospective students is available online at http://www.utexas.edu/visitors/. This site includes links to campus maps and a variety of guided and self-guided tours. Visitor Center: (512) 471-1000; Undergraduate Admissions Center: (512) 475-7440.

Museums

Harry Ransom Center
21st and Guadalupe
Street
(512) 471-8944
http://www.hrc.utexas.edu/
Open Tuesday through Sunday
Admission is free

Lyndon Baines Johnson Library
and Museum
2313 Red River Street
(512) 721-0200
http://www.lbjlibrary.org/
Open daily except Christmas
Admission is free

Blanton Museum of Art
Martin Luther King Boulevard
and Congress Avenue
(512) 471-7324
http://www.blantonmuseum.org/
Open Tuesday through Sunday
Admission fee

Texas Memorial Museum (Texas
Natural Science Center)
2400 Trinity Street
(512) 471-1604
http://www.utexas.edu/tmm/
Open daily except major holidays
Admission is free

The Forty Acres

In 1839, the Congress of the Republic of Texas designated a tiny hamlet on the banks of the Colorado River as the site for its capital and renamed it for Stephen F. Austin, the founder of Anglo-American Texas. The act specified that land be set aside for a public university but little more was done over the years as the independent republic joined the United States, seceded to join the Confederacy, and gained re-admission to the U.S. after the Civil War. Finally, the Texas constitution of 1876 mandated the state legislature to establish and support "a university of the first class." Following a referendum that affirmed Austin as the seat of the institution, with a separate branch in Galveston as a medical school, the University of Texas opened its doors in 1883.

The university's eight faculty members and 218 students occupied temporary quarters in town while a permanent building was erected on an outlying hill approximately three-quarters of a mile northwest of the Texas Capitol, then under construction. Designed by Frederick E. Ruffini, a prolific Austin architect, the first portion of the medieval-revival Old Main Building occupied the highest point of the forty-acre site, near its center. It faced the capitol to the southeast, establishing an axis slightly skewed to the city's grid. The siting was inspired, but the initial structure remained an odd fragment

"Partial View of Austin, Texas, 1891," Augustus Koch, delineator. The view exaggerates the size of Old Main at the center of the Forty Acres, which occupies mostly undeveloped land between the city center and the suburb of Hyde Park.

Old Main, 1893

for years until it was finally completed in 1899 after three construction phases directed by three different architects. During this time, it was the only academic building on campus, and, like similar main buildings on campuses across the country in the nineteenth century, it housed all classes, the library, an auditorium, faculty and administrative offices, and even a basement gymnasium.

From the beginning, the university attracted development in the surrounding area. Guadalupe Street, which borders the campus on the west, became the primary location for shops and services catering to student life. Beyond it, the neighborhood known as West Campus was occupied by a mix of single-family homes and boarding houses, a pattern that continued south of 21st Street, and, less densely, to the east of the campus. The promise of the university as a center of high culture, signifying Austin's emergence as "the Athens of the whole South," in the words of an 1893 guidebook, inspired some of the city's leading families to build luxurious homes in the blocks north of 24th Street. Of these, only the Littlefield Home remains. More enduring is the ring of churches and other places of worship and religious fellowship that line the campus along 27th Street, Guadalupe Street, and 21st Street.

Today, the main campus of The University of Texas at Austin covers approximately 350 acres and includes approximately 140 buildings.

Student enrollment has expanded to nearly 50,000 alongside 21,000 faculty and staff. During the peak class changes on Mondays, Wednesdays, and Fridays, the density of pedestrian traffic is arguably higher than that of any city in Texas, and on football Saturdays more than 100,000 people crowd into the stadium. In a state known for its wide-open spaces, sprawling suburban developments, and big cars, the UT campus has been an urban laboratory for testing ways of managing growth and of using design to foster a sense of shared identity among all who study and work there. As a casual walk across the campus reveals, the process has been neither of a single mind nor consistently successful. Disparities of organization, scale, and building type testify to different visions, each expressive of its time. Today, with little land available for further expansion, planners and architects must address the

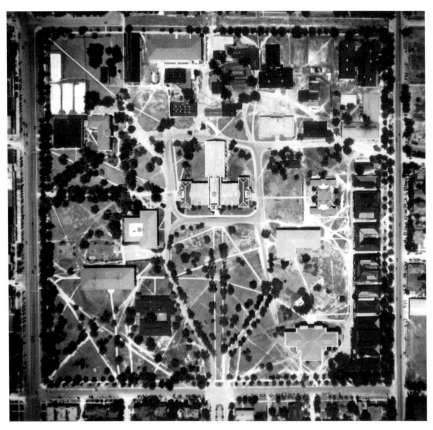

Aerial view of the Forty Acres, 1926. This view shows the tree-lined Peripatos bordering the Forty Acres, efforts to provide a monumental approach to Main Building from the south, with both Battle and Garrison Halls framing the future site of the plaza, and myriad rogue paths. Shacks line the east edge of the Forty Acres and are scattered among the permanent buildings.

changing needs of the university community by integrating new construction within the existing fabric. Similar challenges exist in the surrounding neighborhoods.

Old Main was demolished in the 1930s to make way for the present Main Building with its iconic tower, but surviving traces of other features provide glimpses of the appearance of the campus in its early years. The boundaries of the original tract, known, simply, as the Forty Acres, are clearly visible today: 21st and 24th streets on the south and north, Guadalupe Street and Speedway (originally Lampasas Street) on the west and east. Just to the north of the Texas Union, near 24th Street, is a stand of live oaks believed to be among the oldest trees on campus. Known as the Battle Oaks in honor of Professor William J. Battle, who was instrumental in their preservation, they are remnants of the groves of oaks and mesquites that once dotted the Forty Acres, which, otherwise, was covered by native grasses and wildflowers long since replaced by manicured lawns.

Although outside the Forty Acres, Waller Creek was another defining feature of the landscape. More so than now, students at the turn of the twentieth century sought out its shade as a refuge from the heat and the vigilant eyes of faculty who took the concept of in loco parentis to heart. The oldest designed feature on campus is not a building but the Peripatos, a tree-lined promenade laid out in 1891 along the perimeter of the Forty Acres.

View of the University of Texas from University Avenue, ca. 1905,
from left to right: Woman's Building, Chemical Laboratory, Old Main Building,
Engineering Building (now Gebauer Building), and B. Hall

Its trace may be seen most clearly along 21st Street to the south of the Harry Ransom Center. The stroll around the "Perip" was a courting ritual for couples with few options for getting away from campus in the days before the automobile.

The character of the early campus in the first decade of the twentieth century was a picturesque park, similar in aspiration to the landscaping of the State Capitol grounds but a poor relative in terms of realization. As at the Capitol, a central tree-lined drive led from 21st Street to Old Main and the grounds were planted with ornamental trees and shrubs and crossed by meandering paths. At the top of the hill, Old Main dominated a loose arrangement of flanking buildings in a variety of medieval-revival and classical styles of which only the Engineering Building (now the Gebauer Building, 1904) survives. The others consisted of a heating plant (1889, demolished 1910); the men's dormitory, Brackenridge Hall, fondly known as B. Hall (1890, demolished 1952); the Chemical Laboratory (1891, demolished 1926); and the Woman's Building (1903, demolished 1959). Down the hill at the southeast corner of the Forty Acres was the Law Building (1906, demolished 1972).

Lacking a plan for the placement of future buildings, the university turned for assistance in 1903 to San Antonio architects Coughlin and Ayres, whose principals, individually or in partnership, designed the Woman's

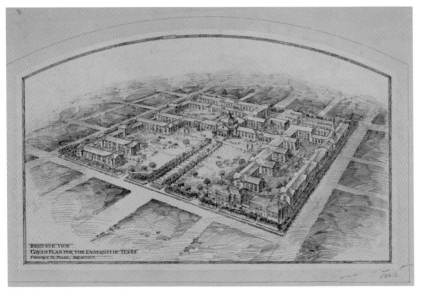

"Bird's-Eye View Group Plan for the University of Texas," Frederick M. Mann, ca. 1909

Building, the Engineering Building, and the Law Building. The firm proposed a plan that would have distributed buildings loosely around the perimeter of the campus, but this scheme did not satisfy the aspirations of President David Houston (appointed in 1905) and long-time regent George Brackenridge. They began a search for a nationally respected architect to create a more memorable master development plan.

By 1909 the university, now led by President Sidney Mezes, selected Frederick M. Mann, head of the Department of Architecture at Washington University in St. Louis where David Houston had become chancellor in 1908. Besides his connection to Houston at Washington University, Mann had become known to members of the UT community in 1907 when Professor Battle recommended him for the design of the University Methodist Church that was to be built just north of the campus, at Guadalupe and 24th streets. Mann received the commission, and the compact Romanesque Revival church with its prominent lantern, tower, and broadly overhanging red tile roofs was completed in 1909.

Despite this auspicious introduction to Austin and a subsequent commission of note in 1910 for the University YMCA (demolished 1970) on Guadalupe and 21st streets, Mann's relationship with the university did not flourish. He built only one structure on campus, the 1910 Power Plant on Speedway (demolished 1977), and the university administration quietly put aside his master development plan. The plan called for the demolition of all but the two most recent buildings on campus, the Engineering Building and the Law Building. Old Main was to be replaced by a classically inspired structure. The other campus buildings were to be arranged as a U-shaped ensemble enclosing the campus on three sides and framing a broad lawn oriented toward the Capitol. The scheme would have replaced the picturesque aesthetic of the original campus with a much more regularized and formal character.

The Cass Gilbert Years, 1909–1922
Mann's scheme was coherent but failed to inspire the university's leadership. Even as he worked on it and plans for the Power Plant in 1909, President Mezes and his advisors were looking elsewhere for an architect who could set forth a more compelling vision for the campus and also design the most pressing building on their agenda: a free-standing library. Influential friends of the university, including Mezes's brother-in-law, the prominent political operator and businessman Edward M. House, made contact with Cass Gilbert in New York soliciting his views on campus design.

Fifty years of age, Gilbert had reached a peak of maturity in his career. Having previously won prestigious competitions for the design of the

Minnesota State Capitol and the U.S. Customs House in New York, he directed a practice, national in scope, that had produced a comprehensive development plan for the University of Minnesota, and projects for public and commercial buildings in Ohio, Michigan, and Missouri, as well as in New York. Respected by his peers, he served as president of the American Institute of Architects in 1908.

The University of Texas had finally found a nationally known architect with the vision to create an enduring image for the campus and the institution. Gilbert imagined an urban campus with well-defined malls, courts, and plazas. Rigorously ordered outdoor spaces defined by arcades and formal plantings replaced the rural green lawns of previous schemes. In January 1910, the Board of Regents designated Gilbert the University Architect and approved his preliminary scheme for the University Library (now Battle Hall, 1911). He held the position for twelve years. Although he would realize only one other commission, the Education Building (now Sutton Hall, 1918), his two buildings and the master plan upon which their placement was predicated have had a long-lasting influence on the planning and architecture of the campus.

Four powerful features set Gilbert's plan apart from its predecessors. First, it called for replacing Old Main with a much larger and more imposing classical building called University Hall. The persistent absence of funds for its construction, although disappointing, provided Gilbert with the time and opportunity to consider at least three distinct architectural approaches for the building. Two were inspired by his projects for the University of Minnesota. One was a grand, domed, neo-baroque structure studied in sketches as early as February 1909 and as late as October 1920. The other was a rectangular building with a dominant colonnade and gabled roof that Gilbert sketched as early as January 1910 and much later as well. The third scheme for University Hall, sketched in 1920, introduced a tall tower rising from a low base. These projects established the idea of a very large building, prominent on the Austin skyline, which would serve as an iconic symbol for the university.

The second distinguishing feature of Gilbert's plan involved the creation of four malls leading down the hill from University Hall in approximately cardinal directions. Of these, the South Mall was the most prominent. It began at a broad plaza facing University Hall. Gilbert locked in the location and scale of the plaza when he built the University Library (Battle Hall) at its western edge. From the plaza a tree-lined lawn and roadways descended to 21st Street flanked by arcades loosely inspired by the porticos Thomas Jefferson had designed along the Lawn of the University of Virginia. Gesturing toward the Capitol, this grand ensemble of University Hall, Main Plaza, and South Mall visually stretched the realm of the campus

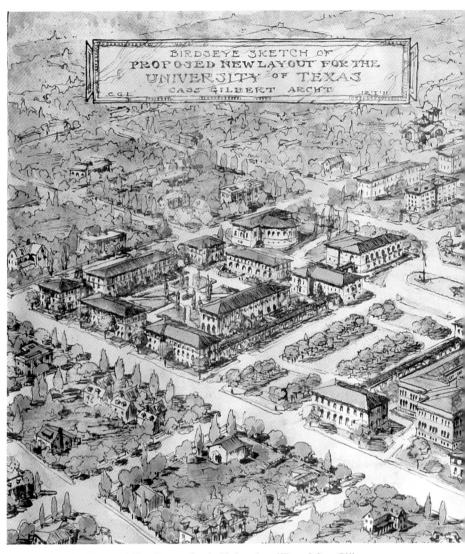

"Birdseye Sketch of Proposed New Layout for the University of Texas," Cass Gilbert, 1911

beyond the Forty Acres and projected a signature presence of the University of Texas as a strong, confident institution. The other three malls made important connections and contributed to a sense of clarity and coherence for the campus. The East Mall and West Mall terminated at well-defined campus gateways on Guadalupe Street and Speedway, respectively.

The shorter North Mall was about as broad as it was long, giving it a less directional character than the others, but its axial walkway and flanking pavilions at 24th Street maintained focus on University Hall. Contrary to the previous development plans for the campus, Gilbert's axes indicated multiple connections to the city growing around it and provided ready options for

expansion beyond the Forty Acres. At the same time they exuded an aura of order, stability, and permanence.

A third feature of Gilbert's plan, which would have lasting significance, focused on the creation of a more intimate, personal scale for the campus. Within the quadrants created by the cardinal axes, Gilbert envisioned quadrangles contained by carefully aligned, mostly linear buildings. He planned the Education Building (Sutton Hall) as the northern edge of the southwest quadrant and built it as a model to guide future development. The space within each of the four quadrants was to have a distinct character, but all were to be less monumental than the malls. These courts were settings for the everyday academic life of faculty and students. They complemented the malls in projecting the dual role of the university as both a powerful institution and a nurturing place of learning.

The fourth feature of Gilbert's plan that gave it appeal to university leaders over previous efforts had to do with its attitude toward consistency versus inclusiveness in the architectural character of buildings on campus. Whereas Frederick Mann had proposed demolishing all but two of the extant buildings in order to create the cohesion he desired, Gilbert allowed for the retention of all of the existing structures except Old Main. He cleverly integrated B. Hall, the Woman's Building, the Engineering Building, and the Law Building, all with very diverse architectural expression, into his scheme. Even the two buildings he completed for the campus, Battle Hall and Sutton Hall, employed variant vocabularies within the architectural language of classicism. In his proposals for other projects—University Hall, a gymnasium, and an outdoor theater—the range of expression was quite broad and accorded with the circumstances of specific functions and sites.

Gilbert believed campus buildings should be carefully coordinated and proposed the classicism of the Spanish Renaissance as a suitable point of departure for creating a distinct and appropriate character for the University of Texas. In his correspondence with university officials, he argued that it was preferable to collegiate Gothic or generic forms of classicism because of the suitability of its broad, overhanging roofs and patterns of fenestration to Austin's climate, the history of Spanish influence in Texas, and the fact that it had not been overused in other parts of the country.

The Herbert M. Greene Years, 1922–1930
In 1922, the Board of Regents decided to not renew Gilbert's contract. The ostensible reason was disagreement over the terms of his compensation, but other issues precluded efforts to resolve the impasse. Among these was tension between Gilbert and university officials regarding their respective roles in the planning process. William J. Battle alluded to the situation in an account written twenty-six years later. "A delightful man personally, he [Gilbert] was less responsive to the wishes of the local committee than any architect we have had."[1] Evidently, the university's leaders wanted more control and felt confident in their ability to play an active role in the process. They also knew they could draw on a larger and more professionalized pool of architectural talent than had been available in Texas at the beginning of the century.

The appointment for a new campus architect went to Dallas architect Herbert M. Greene, whose firm later became Greene, LaRoche, and Dahl. Greene was born in Pennsylvania and grew up in Illinois where he received his architectural training at the University of Illinois. In 1897, at the age of twenty-six, he moved to Dallas and opened an office. His practice flourished, and by the early 1920s it had expanded to other cities with commissions such as the Scottish Rite Dormitory in Austin, just north of the UT campus, and work for the University of Texas Medical Branch in Galveston. Shortly after his appointment as University Architect, he became the first Texas architect to be named a Fellow of the American Institute of Architects. He was talented, efficient, and, not so incidentally, a good friend of Sam Cochran, then chair of the Board of Regents.

Greene stepped into a complicated situation. For a dozen years, Gilbert's master development plan had remained on paper, and his two buildings were the only new permanent academic structures even though enrollment had more than tripled to 4,672 by the time of his departure. Instead of attending classes in the elegant quadrangles Gilbert had envisioned, students received much of their instruction in two dozen wooden temporary buildings arranged in rows along Speedway and dotted elsewhere around the campus. The first was erected in 1911, and most of the others were built during World War I when the university served as a military training center. University administrators deliberately kept the structures unpainted and as rudimentary as possible to remind visitors and, especially, state legislators, of their temporary nature. Their appearance inspired the term "Shackeresque" to characterize UT's architecture of the 1910s.

Shacks along Speedway, 1920s. The Law School rises behind the row of temporary classroom buildings.

The inadequacy of the instructional facilities was matched by a shortage of on-campus housing. B. Hall for men, built in 1890, and the 1903 Woman's Building were the only dormitories. Most students lived in boarding houses and rented rooms in the surrounding neighborhoods.

The underlying cause of these problems was chronic underfunding of the university due to statehouse politics and to a structural flaw in the financing model, which depended on earnings from an endowment of over two million acres of state-owned land in West Texas. The income from grazing and mineral rights was insufficient to meet operating expenses and support ambitious building programs; like many of the state's citizens in the early twentieth century, the university was land rich and cash poor.

When Greene accepted the position of University Architect in 1922, he and his employers had little reason to suspect that this state of affairs would change dramatically. That assumption fell by the wayside just one year later when oil was discovered on university property in Reagan County, and the value of the West Texas leases skyrocketed like a gusher.

Another lingering problem facing the new University Architect in 1922 was the aftermath of a conflict precipitated from the graves of the university's two largest donors who had died within two months of each other in 1920. For years, George Washington Brackenridge and George Washington Littlefield had vied to outdo each other in their largesse toward UT. Brackenridge, a resident of San Antonio, had served as a regent for twenty-seven years, and his financial contributions included the cost of B. Hall on the Austin campus and a dormitory for women at the university's Medical Branch in Galveston. His dream, however, was to engineer the relocation of the main campus from the Forty Acres to five hundred acres of land he had acquired along the north bank of the Colorado River (now Lady Bird Lake) to the west of the city's central business district.

Littlefield, a regent for nine years (two of which overlapped Brackenridge's final appointment) lived with his wife, Mary, in a grand house that survives today at 24th Street and Whitis Avenue. His philanthropic activity included the creation of an endowment for a research collection on Southern history, the Littlefield Collection, which established the university as a major center for historical study. Virulently opposed to Brackenridge's notion of moving the campus (and receiving credit for it), he wrote his will to grant the university over one million dollars in assets providing that the campus remain in its original location.

Following the deaths of Littlefield and Brackenridge, university president Robert Ernest Vinson, a proponent of the new location for the campus, sought to carry out the plan but ran into stiff opposition from those who favored cash-in-hand to the unknown costs of the move. In the end, Littlefield's camp prevailed and the campus remained on the Forty Acres, but the legislature appropriated funds for the university to purchase property for expansion to the north and east.

To plan this expansion, the regents in 1923 retained James M. White, a faculty member at the University of Illinois with considerable experience with planning and supervising construction on that campus. The following year, they named Robert Leon White (no relation to James M. White) Supervising Architect with responsibility for the execution of the buildings Herbert M. Greene would design. As an alumnus and faculty member of the Department of Architecture, White knew the campus well, and his institutional memory would serve the university for thirty-four years.

As the university assembled its design team, it formalized procedures for communicating with it by making permanent the formerly ad hoc Faculty Building Advisory Committee. The committee's responsibility was and remains to advise the president on campus planning and the design of buildings and major renovations. From 1922 until 1948, the committee chair was Dr. William J. Battle, Professor of Classical Languages. A native of North Carolina, Battle had arrived in Austin in 1893 with a freshly minted Ph.D. from Harvard and found his calling at the fledgling university, then barely a decade old. In addition to teaching generations of students the rudiments of Greek and assembling a collection of plaster casts of Greco-Roman sculpture (now in the Blanton Museum) to help them better visualize the ancient world, Battle held administrative positions, including Acting President (1914-1916). His interest in architecture went beyond academic knowledge of its history, and he championed good design on campus and in the community through service on building committees and planning commissions. The shack-strewn campus of the early 1920s must have pained him greatly, and he worked tirelessly as chair of the Faculty Building Advisory Committee to transform the Forty Acres into a place memorable for something more than unpainted wood and tar paper.

Gilbert's departure, the arrival of new personnel and administrative procedures and the newly acquired land, prompted rethinking of the master development plan. James White prepared a number of widely differing proposals, which have recently been identified in the university's archives by Jim Nicar. Among them is a 1923 scheme, briefly approved by university officials, that would have removed all buildings except Battle and Sutton Halls and reoriented the campus to the east with an expanded Battle Hall at the head of a vast mall descending to Waller Creek. Although the university soon rescinded its approval and never fully implemented any of White's other proposals, his plans have had a lasting significance in two respects.

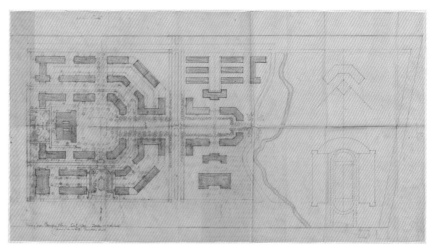

*"Univ. of Texas Campus Plan," James M. White, October 18, 1924. White
proposed doubling Battle Hall to make it the terminus of a grand mall extending
eastward to Waller Creek.*

On the Forty Acres they set the maximum dimensions for the present East
Mall by locating Garrison and W. C. Hogg halls, built by Greene and Paul
Cret, respectively; framed a north axis at 24th Street with the Biological
Laboratories (Greene) and Painter Hall (Cret); and, along Guadalupe
Street, suggested building footprints that would later serve Cret as points of
departure for the Texas Union and the Architecture Building. Beyond the
Forty Acres, White's plans located Littlefield Dormitory and Anna Hiss
Gymnasium for women to the north, Gregory Gymnasium on Speedway,
and the stadium to the east of Waller Creek. These buildings became
generators for the next master development plan that would be prepared in
the 1930s.

Herbert Greene's work on campus was significant for its quantity—
twelve buildings—and quality. His classroom buildings, such as the
Biological Laboratories, Garrison Hall, and Waggener Hall, skillfully
adapted the Renaissance palazzo format of Gilbert's Sutton Hall to difficult
sites and different programs. Greene and his project architects, notably
George L. Dahl, a rising star among Dallas architects who joined the
firm in 1926, worked closely with Battle and supervising architect Robert
Leon White (who had written his UT master's thesis on Spanish colonial
architecture in Texas) in devising ornament inspired by the history and
cultures of Texas and campus life. Greene broke new ground in the robust,
vaguely Lombard Romanesque architecture of Gregory Gymnasium, which
demonstrates his willingness and ability to employ a variety of styles and
materials as a means of creating landmarks and particularizing exceptional

functions. By early 1930, with the design of most of his UT buildings complete, Greene's health began to fail. Although his contract as University Architect was not due to expire until 1933, his direct role in the work became greatly curtailed. He died in February 1932, leaving his firm to complete the final year of the contract. Meanwhile, another figure had entered the stage.

The Paul Cret Years, 1930–1945

In March of 1930, the Board of Regents engaged Paul Philippe Cret as Consulting Architect responsible for the preparation of a new master development plan for the campus. Cret replaced James M. White, who had not retained the confidence of Battle and the chairman of the Regent's Building Committee, Edward Randall. Before hiring Cret, they had offered the position to Philadelphia architect Charles Z. Klauder, the author of a notable text on campus planning and the designer of the development plan and buildings for the University of Colorado at Boulder, which Battle admired as an effective expression of regional identity. Klauder had declined the offer, and Battle and Randall had considered Charles A. Platt of New York and Myron Hunt of Los Angeles before settling on Cret.

Fifty-four years old in 1930, Cret was among the most prominent architects of public buildings in the United States. He had received his architectural training in the Beaux-Arts academies in his native Lyon and in Paris and had immigrated to Philadelphia in 1903 to take up a position teaching architecture at the University of Pennsylvania. A renowned studio critic, he served on the faculty there for thirty-four years instructing generations of architects including future American master Louis Kahn. Cret's notable architectural works began with his winning competition entry of 1908 for the Pan-American Building (now Organization of American States Building) in Washington, D.C., and included the Indianapolis Public Library (1917), the Detroit Institute of Arts (1920–1927), and the Folger Shakespeare Library in Washington, D.C. (1922–1932). His consulting work for universities included development plans for the University of Wisconsin (1911–1914), Brown University (1925), and the University of Pennsylvania (1925).

Battle quickly formed a close rapport with Cret and described the architect as "not only an able designer, he was also a man of the most exquisite taste, & had a charming personality."[2] Cret read widely and had an impressive professional library, which has been divided between the architecture libraries at the University of Pennsylvania and UT. He and Battle interspersed their conversations about the campus with talk of Greek archaeology. Moreover, they shared an evolutionary approach to architectural change. Cret's well-articulated, nuanced positions on this point were

Aerial view of UT *campus, ca. 1937. The view taken shortly after the completion of the new Main Building shows the rapid transformation of the campus in the 1930s.*

informed not only by his mastery of classical design principles but by a profound understanding of the challenges to that tradition posed by the recent work of modernist architects such as Walter Gropius and Le Corbusier.

In June 1931, a year into his contract for the master development plan, the Board of Regents hastily awarded Cret a second contract to design ten new buildings on the campus. This extraordinary commission was prompted by the creation of the Permanent University Fund by the Texas Legislature in April 1931 that greatly increased the university's ability to utilize income from its oil leases. The regents, fearful that the legislature might reduce the funding formula when it met again in 1933, took the architect they had at hand and moved forward quickly to get the new buildings underway.

Cret addressed the commission by establishing four distinctive architectural vocabularies that he would extend to the nineteen buildings for which he was Consulting Architect from 1931 to his death in 1945. Like Gilbert and Greene before him, Cret knew large campuses—as UT would eventually become—required architectural diversity. In a report written to the regents in 1933, he advocated buildings "related, to be sure, but independent, and requiring a certain variety of treatment, to avoid the

monotony and the 'institutional' character inherent to the repetition of
similar units."[3]

The first of the vocabularies Cret employed was a clear outgrowth from
the palazzo-based work of Gilbert and Greene in academic buildings such as
Sutton Hall, the Biological Laboratories, Garrison Hall, Waggener Hall, and
the Chemistry Building (now Welch Hall). Cret's Physics Building (1933,
now Painter Hall) had the limestone base, brick midsection, and elaborate
bracketed eaves with red tile roof that was, by then, well established on the
campus. The contemporary Geology Building (now Will C. Hogg Building)
gave Cret the opportunity to use the same sort of department-specific theme
that Greene had employed. Over the following decade, he utilized this
vocabulary with some significant variations on six other campus buildings,
ranging from residence halls such as Carothers Hall (1937) to academic
buildings for Chemical Engineering and Petroleum Engineering (1942).

The second vocabulary Cret employed was more rugged and varied
in massing and employed brick as the dominant building material. He
used it for three dormitories for men in the vicinity of Greene's Gregory
Gymnasium: Brackenridge Hall (1932), Roberts Hall (1936), and Prather
Hall (1937).

Cret's third vocabulary was also characterized by informal massing
with buildings assembled as collections of separate, sometimes juxtaposed,
volumes. These buildings, however, featured all-stone facades rather than
brick, which had become a dominant material in every new campus building
since Sutton Hall. Three of Cret's best works, the Home Economic Building
(now Mary E. Gearing Hall), the Architecture Building (now Goldsmith
Hall), and the Texas Union—all of 1932—define this genre. All are composed
of two-, three-, and four-story elements sheathed in a combination of
smooth, Cordova Cream limestone and random ashlar fossiliferous Cordova
Shell limestone, both of which were quarried in the Austin vicinity. This
group of buildings created a fresh new look for the campus, distinct from
but compatible with the simple stereometric volumes, palazzo compositional
format, and materials treatments of Cass Gilbert's seminal landmarks nearby.

Cret's fourth vocabulary was also a new invention for the campus.
Reserved for the most monumental buildings and ensembles, he called this
vocabulary "New Classicism," dominated as it was by traditional features
of classical composition, such as symmetry and regularity, but restrained
in the use of ornament. The most prominent example of this vocabulary
is the Main Building, planned to house both the library and the university
administration and constructed in two phases in 1931 and 1937. Conceived
as the new centerpiece of the campus and a counterpoint to the dome of the
Capitol Building, Cret's Main Building replaced Ruffini's Old Main and

boldly proclaimed the university as a beacon of higher education in Texas. Cret designed two other buildings in the "New Classicism" vocabulary: Hogg Auditorium (1933), and the Texas Memorial Museum (1937).

Supported by oil-lease revenue supplemented by allocations of federal Public Works Administration funds for five dormitories and the new Main Building, the campus building boom provided a boost to Austin's economy during the difficult years of the Great Depression. The rapid pace of construction required a well-defined process for design and supervision. Cret's contract with the Board of Regents specified his responsibility for providing the preliminary designs for all buildings and supervising the preparation of final plans and specifications, which were to be assigned either to the firm of Greene, LaRoche and Dahl or to Robert Leon White.

Battle and the Faculty Building Advisory Committee worked closely with Cret and the other architects on a host of issues ranging from the organization of classrooms to the iconography of architectural ornament. Battle reviewed drawings with a sharp eye and no little pleasure. For example, on October 8, 1931, he fired off a telegram to Cret, "Please restudy south entrance Geology [W. C. Hogg Building]. Upper part does not seem happy." Cret replied a week later:

> Regarding the door of Geology, I may be following too much in some details, the picturesque, and I might say, illiterate character of the early Spanish Renaissance, or the Colonial Spanish. This leads me to forget, on purpose, the Classic or Italian arrangements. I believe that, granting that the full size study by the Architects [Robert Leon White with Greene, LaRoche and Dahl] is made in the same spirit, it will give to the buildings, a distinctive character.[4]

The subject of this exchange may have been only an entrance detail, but Cret's words say much about his approach to the architectural character of his buildings at UT. He followed Gilbert and Greene in using Spanish Renaissance and Spanish colonial architecture as a point of departure for campus buildings. The "illiterate character" of these styles (compared to Italian and French classicism) also may have appealed to him as expressions of the frontier, where necessity and distance from centers of high culture inspired creative departures from entrenched doctrines. For some buildings, such as those using random ashlar limestone (such as Gearing Hall), his appreciation of the old stone houses of Austin also entered the mix. In adapting these historical design motifs to modern buildings, Cret's goal was not to replicate the past but to foster the university's identity as a unique place.

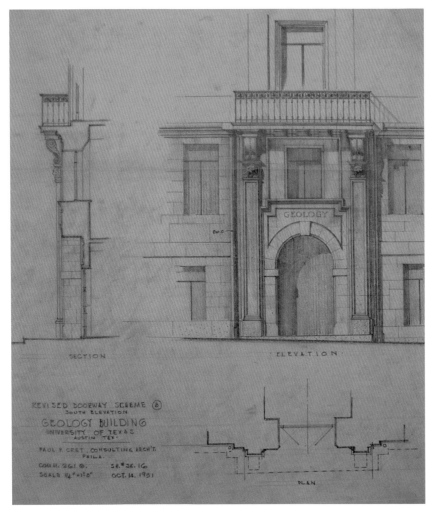

"Revised Doorway Scheme B, South Elevation, Geology Building," Paul Cret,
October 14, 1931. Study for the entrance to the Geology Building (now W. C.
Hogg Building) prepared by Paul Cret's office in response to William J. Battle's
criticism of an earlier scheme.

The pressure of designing new buildings slowed, but did not eclipse,
Cret's work on the master development plan for the campus, and he
submitted the completed document to the Board of Regents in January 1933.
It knit his own work together with that of his predecessors. The scheme
respected Gilbert's master plan with malls defining four varied quadrants
where ranges of buildings defined pleasant outdoor rooms. Cret's South
Mall is similar to Gilbert's proposal with double rows of trees along each
side and buildings connected by colonnades, but Cret arranged the buildings
perpendicular to the mall (much as Gilbert had planned for the University of

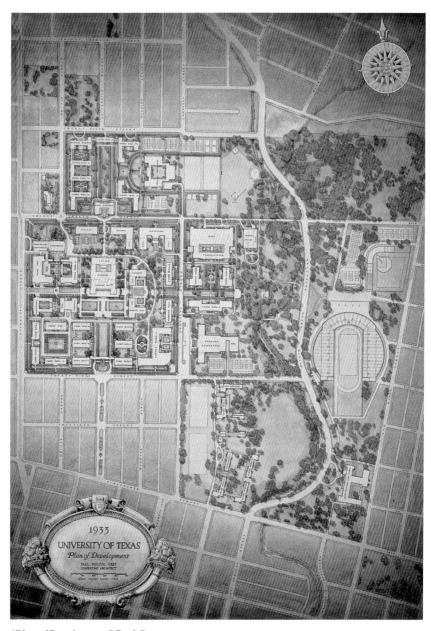

"Plan of Development," Paul Cret, 1933

Minnesota and had suggested in a 1909 sketch for UT). Another departure is a reduction of the mall's width from the 300 feet Gilbert had proposed to 225 feet in order to make the proportions more in keeping with the Great Lawn at the University of Virginia, which Cret admired greatly.

He also responded to the work of Greene and White. Anna Hiss Gymnasium and Littlefield Dormitory became key delineators of a women's campus of dormitories and recreational facilities to the north of the Forty Acres, and Gregory Gymnasium and Greene's buildings for engineering similarly became the centerpieces for open spaces masterfully woven around them.

The formal approach to Main Building along the South Mall from Littlefield Fountain is the iconic feature of Cret's plan, but two other aspects merit attention here because of their significance for long-term development. First is the attention and positive qualities Cret gave to the space between buildings. Such space for him was not an empty void waiting to be filled but an opportunity to create views that link one place with another. These informal areas constitute features of a second aspect of Cret's plan: a gradient from highly formal spaces such as the South Mall and Main Plaza defined by buildings and carefully pruned plantings of trees and shrubs to more park-like settings. Foremost among the latter was Waller Creek, which Cret envisioned as a linear park that would recall the native landscape. This proposal was informed by studies Greene and White had made for the creek and the longstanding interest of Battle and university comptroller John W. Calhoun, in the preservation and expanded distribution of trees on campus, especially live oaks. Besides the trees Calhoun planted, an enduring legacy of his passion is his inventory compiled in 1942, "Trees of the Campus of the University of Texas," that identifies every tree known to have preceded the founding of the university and all plantings since 1905. Cret received additional guidance from the Kansas City landscape architects Hare and Hare, whom the university had retained in 1932.

Cret's work at UT was hampered by illness in the late 1930s and cut short by his death at the age of sixty-nine in 1945. The buildings erected under his supervision and his development plan transformed the campus into a cohesive ensemble and set a high standard for subsequent architects and planners. Battle remained chair of the Faculty Building Advisory Committee until his retirement in 1948. From his aerie on the twenty-seventh floor of Main Building, he could survey the orderly build-out of the classroom buildings and dormitories that he anticipated would speak to students of tradition and a particular sense of place even as they rushed headlong into the future.

Cret's Shadow and the Modernist Challenge, 1945–1960
In 1946, veterans returning from World War II swelled UT's enrollment to 17,260, nearly 7,000 more than before the war. This was the first of successively larger waves of men and women that over the next forty years would increase the student body to what is today approximately fifty thousand. The growth of the student population coincided with an equally

dramatic expansion of the university's research mission, and required both larger and more technologically complex buildings than those erected before the war. A further complication was the emergence of new ideologies of architectural form that called for the invention of a language more expressive of modernity. These demands re-opened questions of architectural image and institutional identity that seemingly had been settled with the acceptance of Paul Cret's master development plan in 1933.

The post–war increase in enrollment was not unexpected. In 1944, President Homer Rainey approved revisions to the master plan that Robert Leon White had prepared with input from the ailing Cret. Its most striking feature was the development of the East Mall beyond what Cret had proposed a decade earlier. In keeping with Cret's original scheme, B. Hall was to be demolished to open the axis from Main Building, and a pendant to Waggener Hall was to be built to frame the mall at Speedway. To the east, symmetrically placed buildings for the College of Engineering were to be attached to the Petroleum and Chemical Engineering Buildings (now Bernard and Audre Rapoport and E.P. Schoch halls) and extend to a large auditorium building that would have terminated the mall shortly before Waller Creek. The plan also called for a new Law School at the southeast corner of the Forty Acres, buildings to complete the southwest quadrant, new dormitories north of Dean Keeton Street where Kinsolving Hall stands today, and a large building for engineering facing the Power Plant across 24th Street. Although few of the proposed buildings would be realized as indicated, the plan remained a guiding reference for the next decade.

In 1948, the regents awarded the position of Consulting Architect to prominent Dallas architect Mark Lemmon. A UT geology graduate who received his architectural training at MIT, Lemmon had built a thriving practice after World War I with large institutional clients including Southern Methodist University and the Dallas Independent School District. During his eight years of service to UT, he had responsibility for fourteen buildings on the Austin campus. Comfortable with historicism, Lemmon sought to maintain a consistent character for the Austin campus faithful to the architectural vocabulary Cret had devised. The programmatic requirements, economics, and construction practices of building in the early 1950s, however, were not those of the 1930s, and many of the buildings realized under his direction are pale reflections of the work of Gilbert, Greene, and Cret.

When Lemmon's plans for the first of his projects became public in 1949, protest by architecture students spread off campus and into the pages of *The Dallas Morning News*. "If the university is to fulfill its role in developing the cultural background of the coming generation," they wrote

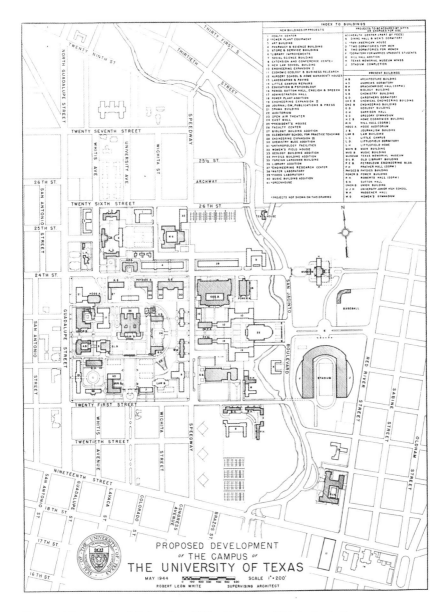

*"Proposed Development," Robert Leon White, May 1944. White's plan indicates
the sites for new buildings infilling the Forty Acres and Women's Campus and,
notably, along the East Mall.*

Business Administration – Economics Building (McCombs School of Business), Page Southerland Page, 1959. View of the west facade shortly after completion in 1962 showing Charles Umlauf's

sculpture, The Family, and the tri-partite organization of office block (left), circulation zone (center), and classroom block (right). The Old Law Building is on the right.

in a letter to the Faculty Building Advisory Committee released to the newspaper, "its entire attitude should be creative, not imitative."[5] They pointed to other universities that were "beginning to build in a free, rational and contemporary feeling" producing works then under construction, such as the Harvard Graduate Center by Walter Gropius and the Architects Collaborative and Baker House by Alvar Aalto at MIT. The controversy did not compel Lemmon to change course immediately, but his position changed over the decade and he employed a modernist vocabulary for his final building on campus, Kinsolving Dormitory (1958).

Lemmon, like Cret, favored an evolutionary approach to modernism, but architectural taste regarding institutional buildings in the 1950s increasingly favored more radical breaks with the past. The appearance of functionality, the absence of traditional ornament, and the prominent display of materials associated with modernity, such as brick, glass, steel, aluminum, and concrete, were hallmarks of the new order. Lemmon and others who had established their reputations as historicist architects struggled to master the new conventions, and younger architects educated in the 1930s and later often took the lead in innovation.

Among the new generation were Louis C. Page, Jr., who earned his bachelor's degree in architecture at UT in 1929 and, like a number of other Texas alumni of the era, went on for graduate study at MIT. There, he encountered Louis F. Southerland, who had transferred from UT to MIT for his undergraduate degree in architecture. Page and Southerland returned to Texas and formed a partnership that added Page's younger brother, George Matthew Page, following his graduation from UT in 1939. Page Southerland Page grew into a large, successful practice in the post-war years with many institutional and governmental clients, and when Mark Lemmon's contract ended in 1956, the regents hired the firm as Consulting Architect. In this capacity Page Southerland Page realized two buildings at the end of the 1950s that furthered the introduction of modernist design on campus. The W. R. Woolrich Laboratories (originally known as the Engineering Laboratories Building) of 1958 is a straightforward expression of its construction—reinforced-concrete frame and brick infill—with no ornament other than the patterns of the colored tiles facing the walls of the entrances. The McCombs School of Business (originally the Business Administration-Economics Building, 1958) was the first modernist building on the Forty Acres. Upon its completion, observers found it strikingly new and innovative, but its design does not ignore the material palette and massing of nearby Waggener Hall. Unlike Lemmon's work that might be described as "Cret-lite," Page Southerland Page sought to rework the ingredients of the older buildings on campus in fresh terms.

Page Southerland Page served as Consulting Architect for only two years, although the firm retained close ties with the university that led to commissions for other buildings on campus. At issue was the regents' reassessment of the role a Consulting Architect should play within the increasingly complex structure of the University of Texas System, which had expanded beyond the Austin and Galveston campuses. No longer comfortable with making a long-term commitment to a single figure or firm, the regents awarded more limited contracts. Jessen, Jessen, Milhouse, and Greeven served as Consulting Architect from 1958 to 1962 followed by Brooks, Barr, Graeber and White from 1962 to 1966. The regents abolished the position of Consulting Architect in 1967, adopting a policy of relying on administrative staff to coordinate the nomination of architects for building projects on a case-by-case basis. From this time to 1994, when the regents commissioned Cesar Pelli to prepare a master development plan, the story of architecture and planning on the campus revolves more around administrators than architects.

The Harry Ransom and Frank Erwin Years, 1960–1975
In the 1960s and 1970s, two giant figures in the university's history occupied center stage: Harry Huntt Ransom, in his capacities as president and chancellor, and regent Frank C. Erwin Jr. Today, Ransom is best known for the great research center that bears his name. He joined the university in 1935 as an instructor of English and rose through the ranks of faculty and administration, becoming dean of the College of Arts and Sciences in 1954 and provost in 1957. After naming him president in 1960, the Board of Regents made him chancellor of the UT system a year later, a position he held until 1971. Highly respected by his faculty colleagues, Ransom also was effective in his dealings with regents and state legislators.

The building honoring regent Frank Erwin, the Frank C. Erwin Jr. Special Events Center, is no less fitting a monument to its namesake than the Ransom Center. Large, confrontational, and resolutely populist, its attributes recall the man whose reputation continues to elicit strong reactions long after his death in 1980. Appointed to the Board of Regents in 1963 by his close friend Governor John Connally, Erwin was a prominent attorney and leader in the Texas Democratic party. He served on the board until 1975, holding the powerful position of chairman from 1966 to 1971.

Erwin was said to have asserted that the greatness of a university rested on buildings, athletics, and funding, and he certainly saw to it that all three flourished on his watch. He was instrumental in the university's most costly building program up to that time and initiated the expansion of athletic facilities that has continued into the twenty-first century. Skillfully exercising his connections in the statehouse, Erwin was instrumental in the nearly tenfold increase in the legislature's appropriations to the university during his service as regent. His friendship with President Lyndon Johnson facilitated the university's access to sources of additional funding in Washington and encouraged the president to locate his library in Austin.

Among the first challenges Ransom faced as president was preparation of a ten-year plan for the university's growth. With enrollment forecasts projecting an additional ten thousand students over the course of the decade (the actual increase would be higher—approximately twelve thousand) and an ambitious agenda to expand research, especially in the sciences and engineering, Ransom sought not only to manage these increases but also to foster academic excellence. To this end he made a pivotal decision that all academic programs would remain on the main campus and only specialized research facilities would be allowed to move to satellites, such as the Brackenridge Tract along Lady Bird Lake or the Pickle Research Campus in north Austin.

The ten-year plan also set the objective that instructional facilities be situated no more than a walk of ten minutes (the interval between classes) from Main Building. Future construction was to be directed to open areas within that radius. The demand for classrooms, laboratories, and offices was such that many of the new structures required larger footprints and significantly greater heights than the older buildings on campus, disrupting the carefully considered proportional and spatial relationships of Cret's master development plan.

Erwin engineered the political and financial apparatus to achieve these new buildings, but his methods compromised his achievements. Among the most dramatic illustrations of his no-holds-barred attitude to opposition is the so-called "Battle of Waller Creek" of October 1969. The conflict erupted over plans to remove trees along a portion of the creek to allow relocation of San Jacinto Boulevard as part the expansion of Memorial Stadium. When word spread that the removal was imminent, students surrounded the site and occupied the trees in defiance of orders to disperse. Erwin went to the scene and personally directed university police to intervene. "Arrest all the people you have to," he has been quoted as saying. "Once these trees are down there won't be anything to protest."[6] Twenty-seven students were arrested, and the trees were destroyed, but other students hauled branches up the hill and piled them in front of the entrance to Main Building to prove him wrong.

Erwin's relentless insistence on expediency evident in the Waller Creek incident applies equally to his approach to architecture. He also relished making big statements, such as Beauford H. Jester Center, which, at the time of completion in 1969, was the largest college dormitory in North America.

Another project led by Erwin made a different sort of statement. In 1976, walls and planters were constructed along the southern and western edges of the Forty Acres facing the commercial districts on 21st Street and Guadalupe Street. They reduced the points of entry to the campus and disrupted the Peripatos (the historic footpath around the Forty Acres) as the campus boundary. Erwin maintained that the barrier was necessary to minimize damage to the landscape by uncontrolled foot traffic, but students and members of the faculty saw the walls as an effort to restrict access to the campus. They argued that he was using architecture as an instrument to inhibit dissent and linked the project to the redesign of the West Mall four years earlier, which had replaced a favorite rally point in front of the Texas Union with a fountain.

Erwin played a prominent role in the expansion of the campus to the east and south. At the time of his appointment to the Board of Regents in 1963, the university's presence east of San Jacinto Boulevard was increasing. Before World War II, the only major buildings in the area were Memorial Stadium, Clark Field, Texas Memorial Museum, and University High School (now the School of Social Work). In the 1950s, Mark Lemmon directed the construction of the new home for the Law School, Townes Hall, on the hill behind the museum and a dormitory (Creekside Residence Hall) below it along Waller Creek. At the beginning of the 1960s, the Art Building was built on San Jacinto and, as a demonstration of the new policy placing service buildings outside the ten-minute-walk zone, the Printing Division Building (now the University Police Building) was situated east of the stadium. Robert Dedman Drive, known then as Red River Street, formed the western edge of a shrinking residential neighborhood platted on a grid of streets. Two blocks to the east was East Avenue, a north-south thoroughfare that became the right-of-way for Interstate Highway I-35, for which construction began in 1952.

The scattered university buildings and the low density of the neighboring private properties made the area a prime target for future development. In addition to providing sites for new buildings, land on the eastern periphery could be used for parking, a problem that had spiraled out of control by mid-century.

The highest-profile project on campus in the era was the Lyndon Baines Johnson Library and Museum and the adjacent Sid Richardson Hall, which extended the campus nearly to I-35. The Johnsons sought a nationally recognized architect and selected Gordon Bunshaft of the New York office of Skidmore, Owings & Merrill, whose Beinecke Rare Books &

MAIN CAMPUS · THE UNIVERSITY OF TEXAS · SPRING 1964

Aerial view of UT *campus, 1964. View of campus looking east shows the university's struggle to accommodate automobile parking. Construction of the East Mall has not yet begun. Beyond the stadium are the remnants of the residential neighborhood that would be razed for the* LBJ *Library complex and other university buildings.*

Manuscript Library at Yale University Lady Bird Johnson admired. Brooks, Barr, Graeber and White, who at the time held the position of Consulting Architect, were named associated architects for the project.

Shortly after the plans for the LBJ complex became public, the university and the city announced their partnership in an urban redevelopment project known as University East that would have extended UT's land holdings across I-35 and deep into the neighborhoods of East Austin. Using federal funds and the power of eminent domain, the city was to acquire the land and transfer it to the university. The predominantly African American residents of the area took exception to the wholesale declaration of blight. Eventually, the university scaled back its plans and concentrated its projects, which eventually included Disch-Falk Field and the first of a complex of service buildings, in the blocks closest to I-35. UT's presence in East Austin, however, remained controversial for twenty years.

A second urban renewal venture during the Erwin years initiated in 1967 encountered less resistance. Known as the Brackenridge Redevelopment

Tract due to its proximity to Brackenridge Hospital on Red River Street,
the site extended from San Jacinto Boulevard to I-35 and from 15th Street to
Martin Luther King Jr. Boulevard (formerly 19th Street), including the Little
Campus. The transformation of the residential neighborhood established a
park along Waller Creek in which the university located the Penick-Allison
Tennis Center and rebuilt Red River Street as a curving drive along an
alignment that allowed the hospital to expand. The massive Frank Erwin
Events Center commands the site, but other notable buildings include the
historic Little Campus, which narrowly escaped demolition, and the new
Collections Deposit Library and Nursing School.

Denouement, 1975–1990
Frank Erwin stepped down from the Board of Regents in 1975, but the last
of the buildings that he had a hand in creating would not be completed for
a half dozen years. Among these were the Perry-Castañeda Library, which
replaced the overcrowded tower of the Main Building as the central library
and the College of Fine Arts complex on the site of Clark Field.

The commissions for these buildings were awarded to a broader range
of firms than had worked in campus during the 1950s and 1960s when the
institution of Consulting Architect was in place. Some firms were not new
to UT. Bartlett Cocke, for instance, who designed the new library, had been
Associate Architect for the Winship Drama Building (1960) during Jessen,
Jessen, Milhouse and Greeven's tenure as Consulting Architect. Cocke, who
received his architectural education at UT (1922) and MIT (1924), was the
principal of a prominent firm in San Antonio that he founded in 1931 and an
established figure in Texas architecture.

Among the relative newcomers was the Dallas firm, Fisher and Spillman,
founded by J. Herschel Fisher and Pat Y. Spillman in 1962. Fisher was a
1936 graduate of UT's architecture program and had followed the well-
beaten path to MIT for graduate study before going into practice in Dallas
after World War II. Spillman was among the first generation of architects
educated after the war. After completing his undergraduate studies at Texas
A&M University in 1949, he went to Harvard University for graduate study in
architecture and then to Yale University to study city planning. He worked for
the prominent Chicago modernist Harry Weese before returning to Texas.

The firm received its first UT commission, the Joe C. Thompson
Conference Center, in 1968 and became dominant on campus in the mid-
1970s with a string of major commissions including the Fine Arts complex,
the Lee and Joe Jamail Texas Swimming Center, and the Recreational Sports
Center. Like Bartlett Cocke's Perry-Castañeda Library, their buildings are
imposing structures characterized by monumental, geometric forms clad in

broad masonry surfaces (brick rather than the library's Indiana limestone) with deeply set fenestration.

The building boom Erwin engineered helped the campus keep pace with the student population that expanded to 40,000 during his terms as regent, but the period of growth was not over—another 10,000 students would be wearing Burnt Orange by the end of the 1980s, adding stress on campus buildings and infrastructure. Seeking new sites for expansion, the university attempted to purchase sixteen blocks in the East Austin neighborhood south of Manor Road known as Blackland in 1982 and threatened reluctant property owners with eminent domain proceedings. As in the late 1960s, the residents, some of whom had been displaced by the university's first expansion in the area, protested, and a bitter dispute raged for six years, until President William Cunningham forged an agreement with the neighborhood association that reduced the planned acquisitions by half.

In the more central areas of the campus, several large new buildings were built in the 1980s, including the University Teaching Center and the Chemical and Petroleum Engineering Building, but the decade is best characterized as a time for renovations to the buildings of the pre–World War II era. The renovation and addition to Goldsmith Hall, home of the School of Architecture, by Thomas, Booziotis and Associates is noteworthy for the sensitive handling of new construction alongside original fabric. At the end of the decade, a distinguished member of the architecture faculty, Charles Moore, reintroduced architectural whimsy, last seen in the buildings of Greene and Cret, in the extension to the Etter-Harbin Alumni Center that he designed with faculty colleague Richard Dodge.

Controversial Missteps and the Pelli Plan, 1990–2010
In 1990, two projects were initiated that highlighted the consequences of building in a piecemeal fashion without attention to the relationship of each part to the whole. University officials announced in August of that year that the east wing of the historic Anna Hiss Gymnasium would be demolished to make way for a new molecular biology building. Architectural historian D. Blake Alexander decried the action in *The Daily Texan* by observing, "We are now getting to the point that we're encroaching upon and actually destroying the strongest element that holds the campus together—the original 1933 plan by Paul Cret.... There is no long-range plan, and without one, the campus will continue to deteriorate."[7] The issue for Alexander went beyond the loss of a historic building to a more general lack of appreciation for the significance the spaces between buildings can have on the quality of the campus. No small part of the beauty of Anna Hiss Gymnasium was its place in the sequence of terraces Cret had laid out from the Littlefield

group of dormitories to Speedway, but over the years they had been whittled away with the addition of new buildings, such as Burdine Hall (1970). The destruction of Anna Hiss Gymnasium's natatorium wing in 1994 removed another piece from the mosaic.

At the same time, students were preparing a referendum to support the creation of a new student services building. After it passed in early 1991, a site was selected north of Dean Keeton Street that was severely compromised by an adjacent decrepit apartment building and by difficult, if not dangerous, pedestrian accessibility. When students saw the resulting "rat-maze" design for the building, they initiated a referendum in late 1993 to withdraw their support. In response, newly installed President Robert Berdahl pledged that a campus plan would be launched that would examine the university's building and land needs to prevent such problems in the future.

By the time a request for qualifications was distributed to dozens of the top architectural and planning firms in early 1994, the ambitions of the new campus master plan had grown well beyond just a land-planning exercise. Unlike the ten-year plan of 1960, which directed growth primarily in quantitative terms, the new effort included qualitative directives to "promote interaction and community" and "identify and define a system of lively, interactive public spaces for the campus which can provide an environment for community exchange."[8] President Berdahl was strongly committed to the planning process and saw the physical design of the campus as a vehicle for making the university a more humane, cohesive, and stimulating community.

A public process of narrowing down the long list of submissions from architect/planners and bringing five of them to the campus for extensive interviews led to the appointment of Cesar Pelli & Associates of New Haven, Connecticut, as the primary master plan consultant. After a fifty-year hiatus the University of Texas had returned to its model from the early part of the twentieth century whereby it invested strongly in a master planning process, which addressed both qualitative and quantitative issues, and sought out top talent to lead it.

The recommendations of the Pelli Campus Master Plan reframed the direction of building on the campus and have made a significant contribution to creating the "sense of community" its framers had envisioned. Even before its formal adoption, it began to positively influence projects like the John B. Connally Center for the Administration of Justice and the renovation of Gregory Gymnasium. Over the next fifteen years, substantial advances were made on all of the plan's various recommendations, and an era of phenomenal growth and physical transformation on the campus was conducted, for the most part, in an orderly, coherent fashion.

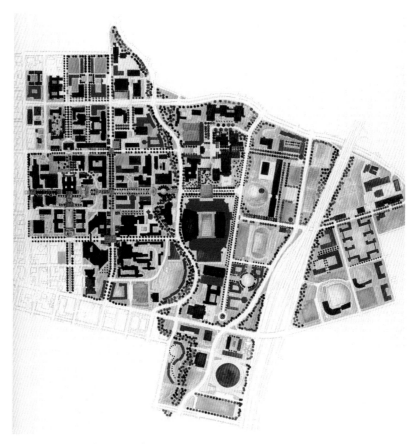

UT *Master plan, Cesar Pelli & Associates, and Balmori Associates, Inc.,*
published 1999

In accordance with the plan, Speedway was closed to all but emergency
vehicular traffic in 1999 and much of the surface parking in the central
campus was gradually relocated to four new parking garages at the periphery.
Pedestrians began to reclaim the central campus in a way that had not been
possible since before World War II. New occasions like "Gone to Texas,"
"Forty Acres Fest," and an enhanced spring graduation ceremony took
advantage of the transformation. Informal demonstrations, festivals, parties,
and performances began to happen more frequently, especially in the plaza in
front of Gregory Gymnasium.

An ambitious redevelopment scheme by landscape architects Peter
Walker and Partners was commissioned in 2006 for Speedway Mall and the
East Mall. The Walker scheme adopted the activity nodes at 21st Street and
24th Street suggested by the Pelli Plan and took its intention for a gracious
ensemble of open spaces on the campus to a higher level of interaction,
beauty, and sophistication.

Two very large, new dormitory complexes, San Jacinto Residence Hall on Waller Creek and Almetris Duren Residence Hall on Whitis Avenue were completed in accordance with the Pelli Plan in 2001 and 2007 respectively. As predicted, they substantially enhanced the twenty-four-hour character of the campus, contributing to both safety and vitality. The plan indicated locations for new recreational activity centers including outdoor swimming pools added to Gregory Gymnasium (2007) and a new Student Activities Center (2010) on the site adjacent to it. Benefitting all students, such social magnets are especially meaningful for those who are just beginning to orient themselves to campus life.

Similar success in consolidating activity, generating an active pedestrian life, and helping to create meaningful open spaces has been had with academic buildings constructed on infill sites in the campus core. The A.C.E.S. Building (2000), Seay Building (2001), North Office Building (2002), Neural and Molecular Science Building (2005), Blanton Museum (2007), and the Belo Center for New Media (2012, projected) all occupy infill sites identified in the Pelli Plan and follow its massing recommendations to define well-formed open spaces around them.

Future Directions

By 2009, the Faculty Building Advisory Committee (FBAC) had begun to identify areas of concern where the Pelli Plan no longer satisfied current needs and advocate a new master plan. In 2008, for the first time a Cret-era building (the Experimental Science Building, completed 1952, designed by Cret's successors Harbeson, Hough, Lingston and Larsen with Broad and Nelson and Robert Leon White) was demolished to make way for the new Norman Hackerman Building (2010). This loss has been followed by the demolition of an earlier Cret building, Taylor Hall (1934, demolished 2011) to provide space for the new Bill and Melinda Gates Computer Science Complex (planned completion in 2012). Neither of these removals of older buildings on the campus to make way for new ones was envisioned in the Pelli Plan. The FBAC called for a comprehensive historical inventory of campus buildings as part the new planning process to be sure the architectural heritage of the campus was appropriately protected. A grant from the Getty Foundation funded a pilot project for such a study on the Forty Acres undertaken by the School of Architecture's Historic Preservation program.

At the same time plans by the City of Austin to improve Waller Creek with active development and hike and bike trails below 15th Street and by the regional transit authority to build a light rail line that might run along San Jacinto Boulevard demanded proactive coordination to be sure that

Experimental Science Building, Harbeson, Hough, Livingston and Larsen, Consulting Architects; Broad and Nelson, Architects, 1951. Behind Experimental Science are Anna Hiss Gymnasium and the women's sports fields, since replaced by science and engineering buildings.

Taylor Hall, Greene, LaRoche and Dahl, Architects; Paul Cret, Consulting Architect, ca. 1935

the campus received the maximum benefit from these transforming urban initiatives. The potential of these efforts to positively impact the east side of campus between San Jacinto Boulevard and I-35 suggested that a new master plan might look for infill sites and growth potential there in a way that could not have been anticipated in the 1990s.

In addition, there was a growing sense among campus leaders that the design guidelines in the Pelli Plan had been interpreted too literally and become a constricting factor preventing the campus from receiving architecturally distinguished buildings. This concern had erupted into polarizing controversy in 1999 during the design of the Blanton Museum of Art when members of the Board of Regents rejected the broad interpretation of the guidelines proposed by Herzog & de Meuron Architekten and insisted on a building with the stylistic traits of the Cret era.

Like many other campuses, the University of Texas is seeking to find the appropriate balance between the creation of a strong, cohesive sense of place and the expression of diversity and progress over time. The next campus master plan will need to set a map for how that might be accomplished in the next chapter of the university's development.

WALK ONE: THE FORTY ACRES

Standing on the steps of the Main Building and looking out over its plaza to the State Capitol beyond is one of the most memorable urban views in Texas. This is the ceremonial heart of the university. It is where freshmen are welcomed to The University of Texas at Austin before their first day of classes and where graduation is held with huge crowds and great fanfare each spring.

The three buildings facing the Main Plaza are excellent illustrations of the three early eras of the campus' development. Cass Gilbert's twelve-year tenure as campus architect is beautifully portrayed by Battle Hall to the west, the grand old dowager from which much of the university's architecture emanated. Herbert Greene's era is represented by Garrison Hall to the east, one of his best efforts at "regionalizing" Gilbert's vocabulary to Texas. Paul Cret's Main Building to the north illustrates the successful climax of his grand vision for the university and the rich, iconic imagery he developed to describe the aspirations of an ambitious institution. All three buildings have the powerful individual imprint of their talented architects and their distinctive eras but also work together gracefully to create a memorable urban space.

Few campus visitors or even long-time campus inhabitants realize that the six buildings that flank the South Mall at the base of the Main Plaza are relative newcomers. The first of the group known as "The Six-Pack" was not begun until the 1940s, and the last was not finished until 1968. Although the Littlefield Fountain, the double row of live oaks, and the buildings that define the mall all seem cut-of-the-same-cloth, their history involved many different actors in a drama that played out over a long period of time.

Likewise, the West Mall took many decades to reach the richness and completeness it has today. From 1910 to the 1930s it was a broad, ill-defined open space with a far-flung collection of disparate, often temporary buildings. From the 1930s to the 1960s it was a snaggle-toothed battleground between structured urbanity and leftover gaps and holes. Flawn Academic Center, completed in 1963, provided definition to the mall's north edge, and the openness of its terrace and ground floor populated by students day and night continue to animate the space today.

Throughout the Forty Acres a similar story is played out over and over. Incremental construction finally congeals into lovely, well-conceived urban spaces. Gilbert, Greene, and Cret conspired over more than twenty-five years to create the Main Plaza. Six different firms over three-and-a-half decades defined the beautifully coherent South Mall. Seven firms over more than five decades worked to complete the West Mall. Eight firms over a similar span of time contributed to the creation of the restful plaza in front of the Harry Ransom Center.

Unlike many other universities where a single architect might control a district of the campus and complete a coherent group of buildings over a relatively short span of time, the University of Texas' campus architects spread their work broadly and almost never completed an ensemble they had begun.

Cass Gilbert's two buildings turned their backs on each other, seeding two different campus groups rather than concentrating on one. Herbert Greene scattered his twelve projects across the Forty Acres and beyond. No two buildings faced each other or even faced a common quadrangle. Even Paul Cret's nineteen projects over a decade and a half tended to complete groups started by his predecessors (like the buildings around the Main Plaza) or start a group he would leave to others to finish (like the South Mall).

The eventual success of the Forty Acres in achieving a lively, coherent, well-proportioned series of building ensembles and open spaces must therefore be credited to the quality of the campus' master plans and to the fidelity to them demonstrated by dozens of architects over the last century. Though individual buildings in the campus core are often extraordinary in their own right, the most impressive aspect of the Forty Acres is the way in which individual buildings add up to become more than the sum of the parts and create worthy crucibles for campus life.

1. Battle Hall
Cass Gilbert, 1910

When construction began on a long-awaited new library building in April 1910, a landmark architectural era commenced at the University of Texas. Cass Gilbert's bold departure from previous campus design set the tone for four decades of UT buildings and provided a benchmark by which the best architectural achievements at the university would be measured well into the twenty-first century.

The *University Record* noted at the time, "The style and materials chosen (Spanish Renaissance and cut limestone) are not like those of the older buildings on the campus [e.g. Old Main, B. Hall, Woman's Building, Old Law Building (Pearce Hall)]. It was decided by the Regents, after much consideration, that only by making this departure could the beginning of a beautiful and fitting central group of university buildings be made." Those who helped shape the design of the new library considered the style "naturally induced by the Spanish influence in Texas" and "altogether suitable to the local conditions" since it was developed in a country with a similar climate.

The general format of the library is that of a Renaissance palazzo, characterized by a heavy ground floor pierced by spare, plain openings with a much grander *piano nobile* above. After studying alternatives varying in proportion and number, Gilbert filled the principal facade of the *piano nobile* with seven large, arched openings. A single arched opening punctuated each of the end facades. An eccentrically large, hipped roof with deep overhangs capped the composition and provided a shadowy space below for a richly ornamented soffit.

Dressed Cordova Cream limestone from nearby Cedar Park dominated construction of the library walls. A denser granite base joined the walls to the ground in order to prevent moisture from rising through the soft local limestone. (Where renovations violated this rule on the south side, the rising damp has produced noticeable damage.) Red barrel tiles, strikingly uniform in color, sheathed the prominent roof. Polychrome terra-cotta lent additional color and detail around the arched openings and on roundels placed between the upper-floor windows. Finely crafted wrought iron gave form to balconies and lamps.

The ornament of Battle Hall is particularly fine and well-suited to the purpose of the building. The terra-cotta window surrounds depict books as well as torches and lamps (symbols of illumination and enlightenment). Owls, representing wisdom, are prominent both in the window surrounds and as overburdened supporters of the brackets under the eaves. Signs of the zodiac are represented in the roundels beginning with Aquarius at the southwest corner and continuing around the building in the order of the calendar through Capricorn at the northwest corner. The colorful eight-foot-deep soffit with its elaborate coffers was painted under the direction of

Battle Hall

Elmer Garnsey, a New Jersey artist who had worked with Gilbert on the Minnesota State Capitol and the New York Customs House.

Having experienced structural problems in the Old Main building, the university was committed to permanence and freedom from repair in this new venture. Concrete foundations extended to bedrock (forty feet down in some cases) and were described as "uncommonly thick." Masonry load-bearing walls held up floors and a roof of reinforced concrete supported on steel. Not only was the new look of the building meant to establish a more lasting vision for the campus, but its construction was also based on a philosophy of building for the long term.

The architectural character of the library owed much to nineteenth-century library precedents such as Henri Labrouste's Bibliothèque Ste.-Geneviève (1851) in Paris and the Boston Public Library (1895) by McKim, Mead & White (for whom Gilbert had worked in his early career). There are also striking similarities to Gilbert's own St. Louis Public Library, the commission for which he had won in a competition in 1907.

Inside, the lower floor of the library had vaulted entry halls separating four long, narrow rooms originally occupied by the president, dean, auditor, and registrar. A gracious wrought iron staircase illuminated by generous northern light led to the *piano nobile* above. At the top of the stair was a sky-lit delivery room where patrons could request and receive books. To the west of the delivery room were five levels of book stacks built of a tightly spaced steel frame with structural marble floor/ceiling slabs. To the east of the delivery room was the architectural tour de force of the library's interior, the reading room.

Perhaps because of its intimacy (along with a remarkable dignity and grandeur) this landmark interior has long been a favorite place to study. The room's simple volume spanned by robust trusses combines with stone walls and graceful arches to create a space that is remarkably comfortable. In the days before air conditioning, its high ceilings and cave-like thermal mass, along with its heavily-shuttered windows and provisions for cross-ventilation, made it much cooler than other campus buildings. Today, this room just *feels* like a traditional academic library, with its heavy casework and tables, its beautifully carved wooden screens, and its general dimness supplemented by task lights illuminating books and students' faces.

When the building was completed, it would have looked like a very odd intrusion on the campus. Its Mediterranean style was a radical departure from the other buildings and would have been particularly jarring next to the Collegiate Gothic Old Main beside it. The library's urbane massing and volume would have seemed teetering and out of place in the undefined pastoral landscape that sloped awkwardly below it. This was a building about the future, and it would be more than two decades before the campus managed to rise to its high standards. Now, of course, like a *grande dame* presiding over her offspring, the library seems perfectly natural and at ease, having shaped a legacy on its own demanding terms.

Battle Hall served as the primary library for the university until 1937 when that function moved to the new Main Building. For a time, it was used by the Fine Arts Department for various purposes and later was the home of the Eugene C. Barker Texas History Center (now the Briscoe Center for American History housed in Sid Richardson Hall). It was named for Dr. William J. Battle, the long-time chairman of the faculty building committee in 1973 and became the home of the Architecture and Planning Library five years later.

2. Garrison Hall

Herbert M. Greene, LaRoche and Dahl, 1926; renovation: 3D/International, Inc., 2008

Named for George P. Garrison, one of the first members of UT's faculty and chair of the history department until his death in 1910, this second building on the campus by Herbert M. Greene demonstrated his ability to capably apply the architectural vocabulary that Cass Gilbert had established in Sutton Hall to make a powerful building on a prominent site in the heart of the campus. Planned to house the departments of history, government, economics, sociology, psychology, and philosophy, Garrison Hall is one of the few lasting indications of the campus master plans prepared by James M. White, who worked alongside Greene in the 1920s. White and Greene envisioned the L-shaped building as one edge of a frame marking the beginning of a wide east mall leading down the hill from a greatly enlarged Main Plaza to Waller Creek. Since this plan was discarded shortly after the design of Garrison Hall was completed, the building looks a bit out-of-kilter with the axiality of the plaza it faces today. Paul Cret, in his Development Plan of 1933, proposed that Garrison's facade be almost doubled in length to make it symmetrical with the center-line of Battle Hall, but that plan was not executed either.

With Garrison Hall, Greene faced a challenge in placing a palazzo-inspired building on a sloping site, similar to what he encountered with the Biological Laboratories. Responding in much the same way, he inserted a foundation floor under a three-story format established by Sutton Hall and faced it with strong horizontal bands of stone with deeply recessed reveals. The L-shape, with its long leg running down the steep slope, aggravated the conflict but also allowed a large amount of floor space with full-sized windows to be placed below the level of the front entrance on the Main Plaza.

From the Main Plaza the manipulation of the ground slope is invisible, and the building reiterates Sutton Hall's ground floor of Lueders limestone with arched openings, topped by two floors faced in brown, tan, and ochre brick. Terra-cotta ornament is used generously, especially on the top floor, to frame and group windows and to animate the building with vivid colors. The hipped red tile roof

Garrison Hall

has deep overhangs with intricate brackets and soffits painted strong colors, complementing those of the terra-cotta.

The themes of the ornament for Garrison Hall make a clean break from its Battle Hall and Sutton Hall precedents and highlight the interests of architect and client in Texas roots. Whereas Gilbert used roundels with zodiac signs for Battle Hall, Greene employed cattle brands in the series of roundels that run under the eaves and between the corner windows. The thirty brands represent most parts of the state and a broad range of time, from the early-nineteenth to the twentieth century. They constitute an effective graphic device for depicting a whole era of Texas history. Among them are the 1833 brand of Stephen F. Austin (west facade, far right window), the "Running W" brand of Richard King, founder of the King Ranch in south Texas (west facade, far left window), and the "LFD" brand of UT benefactor George W. Littlefield (north facade, far right window). They are accompanied by a rich array of other Texana including the names of founders of the Texas Republic and depictions of cacti, bluebonnets, cow skulls, and lone stars interspersed with more classical academic symbols like books, quill pens, and griffins. The north entry portal has an especially fine assembly of these symbols rendered in both terra-cotta and carved stone.

3. Main Building
Paul Cret, Consulting Architect; Herbert M. Greene, LaRoche and Dahl, Associate Architects, 1933, 1937

Paul Cret's powerful centerpiece for the campus was originally planned to house a huge single-purpose central library. As early as 1920, it had become clear that Battle Hall's 250,000-volume capacity was inadequate. The university had rejected Herbert M. Greene's plans for additions, and the matter remained unresolved when Cret was named Consulting Architect. One of his earliest reports to the university, in March 1930, recommended that a new library be built on the top of the hill at the center of the Forty Acres. This vision would not only require enormous sums of money, but also would necessitate the demolition of Old Main Building, which many alumni venerated.

To soften the blow of his grand scheme, Cret suggested that the library be built in three phases, but even before the first-phase library core behind Old Main was completed in 1933, economic stimulus funds from the Depression-era Public Works Administration made it possible to construct the entire ensemble that Cret had planned. Old Main was demolished, and from 1934 to 1937, a U-shaped block was added to the south face of the E-shaped library core, and eighteen floors of additional stack space were placed atop the central leg of the E. The expanded project provided more space than required for the library's immediate needs, and the Board of Regents reassigned, over Cret's objections, most of the south wing for administrative functions. Thus, the structure came to be known as the Main Building, relinquishing its identity as the central library. The vertical stack addition, however, transformed the identity of the building even more significantly and created the most common moniker for the building to this day: The Tower.

The organization of the interior was strongly influenced by its phasing and by the change from its conception as a library to its implementation as a mixed-use building. The earliest E-shaped portion of the ensemble to the north was planned and executed with great orderliness and clarity. On the *piano nobile*, grand reading rooms on the northeast and northwest corners embellished with ornament appropriate to their respective designations, Hall of Noble Words and Hall of Texas, were unified by the delivery room (Hall of the Six Coats of Arms) connected to the stacks in the center.

Main Building

In Cret's original scheme, the U-shaped block would have included a great open stair leading to the delivery room at the heart of the composition. Reading rooms would have occupied the southeast and southwest legs of the U, mirroring the arrangement in the E-shaped block. These wings were to have terminated in outdoor reading terraces—column-lined loggias open to the breeze and offering expansive views on three sides. Located between them, the main reading room would have faced the South Mall and the state capitol. Thus, the stacks, delivery room, and staircase would have been the core for an orderly assembly of five reading rooms wrapping around it.

Main Building, Hall of Noble Words

The redesign of the U-shaped block located offices in the areas intended for the southeast and southwest reading rooms and enclosed the reading terraces for use as classrooms. The main reading room became the Academic Room where the regents met. The ensemble lost its openness, grandeur, and coherent relationship with the pre-existing north section of the building.

Only the top floor was retained for library functions. Three reading rooms dedicated to rare book collections surrounded an elegantly appointed Exhibition Room. To the east, a double-height room finished in walnut paneling and elaborate ironwork housed a collection donated by Miriam Lutcher Stark. To the west was a similar space, but finished in oak and aluminum, originally called the Rare Book Study. Outside each of these spaces were charming roof gardens. To the south of the Exhibition Room was the Wrenn Library, a gift of George Washington Littlefield, with its stained glass windows, alabaster light fixtures, and ceiling murals transferred from their original installation in Battle Hall.

As currently occupied, the U-shaped wing is a rabbit warren of administrative offices with mostly undistinguished rooms and confusing circulation paths. It is a far cry even from Cret's revised vision, although a few vestiges remain. The Academic Room and flanking conference spaces, abandoned by the regents in the 1970s, remain largely intact. The former President's Office on the ground floor is still recognizable although the circulation to it and the suite of spaces around it have lost their original grace. The current presidential suite occupies the former rare book rooms and retains the original interiors, although some of the spaces are jammed with cluttered desks for assistants and administrative personnel.

Main Building's bold, articulate exterior has not suffered the compromises that obscure Cret's intentions for the interior. From the south, the building engages viewers at three, distinctly different scales. The gracious seven-arched loggia at the base presents a welcoming entry at human scale, with its cool, shady cavities, elegant stone detail, and rich wood ceiling. The U-shaped block addresses the monumental scale of Main Plaza, and the tower operates an even bolder scale that commands the entire campus and beyond. The crowning glory, the top of the tower, is an elaborate classical folly that stands in stark contrast to the spare, modern treatment of the shaft itself. An observation gallery above the twenty-seventh floor creates a setback capped by clock faces on each of the four sides. Above the clock faces is a tall belfry that holds a seventeen-bell carillon.

Above the main entrance, the biblical inscription, "Ye shall know the truth and the truth shall make you free" (John 8:32) establishes the theme of Main Building's ornamental program, which celebrates knowledge and learning. Under the windows and beneath the cornices of the northeast and northwest wings are the names of great men of letters in Western civilization and the emblems of twelve notable predecessors of UT—the universities of Bologna, Paris, Oxford, Salamanca, Cambridge, and Heidelberg on the west side and universities of Mexico, Edinburgh, Virginia, and Michigan, as well as Harvard and Vassar, on the east side. On the north face of the tower gold leaf letters indicate five alphabets: Egyptian, Phoenician, Hebrew, Greek, and Latin.

The symbolic power of the Main Building is extraordinary. It has become an icon for the university and an emblem strongly associated with Austin and with Texas. It is the backdrop for graduation every spring and its lighting in various combinations of orange and white proclaims athletic victories, academic accomplishments, and other events of importance to the university community. It is impossible to imagine the University of Texas without the Tower.

4. Sutton Hall

Cass Gilbert, 1918; renovation: Thomas, Booziotis and Associates and Chartier Newton and Associates, 1982

Design for the second of Cass Gilbert's buildings for the campus did not begin until 1915—four years after the completion of Battle Hall. Planned primarily for the School of Education, the building is named for its first dean, William Seneca Sutton, who was also president of the university for a brief time in the 1920s.

The site for what would become Sutton Hall, just southwest of and downhill from Battle Hall, was occupied at the time by one of the many crude temporary

Sutton Hall

buildings on campus, the Home Economics shack. Gilbert placed the new building in accordance with his master plan, as the first unit of a quadrangle anchoring the southwest corner of the Forty Acres. Its main entrance, surmounted by the university seal, faces south towards the proposed courtyard. This orientation explains why, despite their proximity, Sutton Hall has so little formal or functional relationship with Battle Hall, which, instead, addresses what was to become the Main Plaza.

Although both buildings relied on the Renaissance palazzo as a precedent, Sutton Hall differed substantially from its predecessor in scale, material usage, color, and detail. It is faced in a ruddy blend of brown, tan, and ochre bricks. The ground floor is executed in hard, grayish Lueders limestone from West Texas, rather than the Central Texas Cordova Cream that had been used in Battle Hall. Terra-cotta tiles in salmon, blue, green, buff, and white are used to face substantial portions of the facade, creating vertical banks of windows at the ends of the north and south facades and horizontal banks of windows on the top floor on all four sides. The two buildings also differ in their construction. Sutton introduced the reinforced concrete structural frame that later became ubiquitous on campus, whereas the exterior walls of Battle Hall are load-bearing masonry.

The terra-cotta ornament under the eaves and beneath special second-floor windows includes griffins, traditional symbols of vigilance and protection of sacred trusts that may have been chosen with reference to the School of Education, and a weave of ropes and roses—a symbol of connection, completeness, and perfection. Ironically, only one of the rope panels (on the east end of the north face of the building) was installed properly. The rest were set with tiles flipped so that the net of ropes is broken and disconnected.

In 1980, Sutton Hall was extensively renovated for use by the School of Architecture. The general organization of rooms opening off a generous central corridor was retained, but two substantial changes were made to the exterior to facilitate new functions for the building. A new entry portal matching the original south entrance was cut into the north face and a long dormer was added on the north side of the hipped roof to gain mechanical vents and natural light for a newly habitable space in the attic.

Sutton Hall became an important precedent for many campus buildings. The Biological Laboratories and Garrison Hall, built in the next decade, mine it thoroughly both for interior and exterior conformation, materials, and general feeling. Even into the twenty-first century, Sutton Hall's seminal composition of limestone ground floor, brick above, and a red tile roof has become the de facto UT style.

5. Harry Ransom Center

Max Brooks with Jessen, Jessen, Millhouse, Greeven & Crume, completed 1972; renovation: Lake | Flato Architects, Inc., 2003

The original Harry Ransom Center building was variously described as a fortress, monolith, block-house, tomb, or just, "a big gray box." The massive, seemingly windowless seven-story volume on the southwest corner of the campus was considered austere, aloof, uninviting, and even arrogant. The mute walls presented no indication that the building housed one of the foremost assemblies of literary and cultural documents in the world, the realization of professor and administrator Harry Huntt Ransom's ambition to establish a "national library for Texas."

When Lake | Flato Architects were hired to renovate the building in 1999, the center's director, Tom Staley, charged them with giving the building a sense of openness and enhancing awareness of its mission. Though their work was restricted primarily to the lower two floors, the transformation they realized completely altered perceptions about the building and the Ransom Center as an institution.

Two glassy rooms were created at the corners of the entry facade, replacing exterior fountains. One of these rooms accommodates an open stairwell linking the first and second floors; the other is a lobby for an intimate new lecture hall.

Harry Ransom Center

Their double-height glass walls are lined with etched panels containing dozens of images from the HRC's holdings.

At the center of the entry facade the architects also created a glass enclosure for what was formerly a balcony. This allows natural light to spill into a new two-story atrium that greets visitors as they enter the building. The open lobby leads directly into galleries that house changing exhibits of the HRC's treasures. The two permanent artifacts in the space are nested in special cases designed by the architects—a Gutenberg Bible and the world's first photographic image. Throughout the exhibit spaces walls and hung ceilings from the old building have been removed to enable larger volumes and greater display flexibility.

Rich, pecan-paneled walls, walnut floors, and golden Venetian plaster accents complement the original building's palette of concrete and slabs of Cordova Shell limestone. The reading room was moved from a dour, windowless room on the fifth floor to a delightful, light-filled space on the second floor—now one of the most pleasant working spaces on the campus.

"The ugly duckling has turned into a swan," crowed the local Austin newspaper at the completion of the HRC's renovation. The number of visitors to the center increased from eight hundred each month to more than eight thousand. The transformed building allowed the HRC to take on a new role at the university as a place where students, faculty, staff, and visitors can make a real connection with an extraordinary asset that contributes significantly to the university's international status.

6. West Mall Office Building
Jessen, Jessen, Millhouse and Greeven, Consulting Architect; Staub, Rather & Howze, Associate Architect, 1960

Paul Cret's 1933 master plan proposed an addition to the stack wing of Battle Hall that was to house a museum facing Goldsmith Hall. This prime site on the axis linking Sutton Hall and the West Mall remained vacant until 1960, when it was appropriated for a five-story office building. The architects dutifully replicated the broad eaves

West Mall Office Building

(but not the detailing), Cordova Cream limestone, and select moldings of Battle Hall, but the building is characterless, and the tall, west-facing facade acts as a reflector oven that makes the small plaza in front of it nearly uninhabitable in the summer.

Tenants have come and gone over the years. Today, the School of Architecture's University Co-op Materials Resource Center (housing a large, open-shelf collection of building material samples) occupies the West Mall level, and the school's Thermal Lab, a test bed for new types of building envelopes, perches above Inner Campus Drive.

7. Goldsmith Hall

Paul Cret, Consulting Architect; Herbert M. Greene, LaRoche and Dahl, Architects; Robert Leon White, Supervising Architect, 1932; renovation and addition of south wing: Thomas, Booziotis and Associates with Chartier Newton and Associates, 1986

The Architecture Building became Goldsmith Hall in 1978, named for Professor Goldwin C. Goldsmith, a longtime member of the architecture faculty and department chairman during the building's design and construction. Four names are inscribed high on its west facade. Three are familiar to students of art history survey courses: Ictinus, the ancient Greek architect of the Parthenon; Vitruvius, the Roman architect who wrote the oldest surviving treatise on architecture; and Palladio, the Italian Renaissance architect whose treatise continues to inspire architects today. The fourth name, Goodhue, leaves many observers perplexed but offers a key to understanding the aspirations of Cret and other architects working on campus in the 1930s. Best known today as the designer of the Nebraska State Capitol (1922), Bertram Goodhue was a leader among his contemporaries, those seeking an evolutionary approach to adapting traditional architectural principles and forms to the circumstances of modern life. The shock of his untimely death in 1924 was still fresh when Cret and the faculty of the Department of Architecture began planning the first building on campus designed for architectural studies.

Along with the Texas Union, Goldsmith Hall defines the western edge of campus along Guadalupe Street and marks the beginning of the West Mall. Its sturdy tower balances that of the Union and has a corresponding loggia on the top floor. The Roman Doric *aedicula* framing the center window is more austere than the ornament framing the Union's entrance and may have been chosen for its pedagogical significance as one of the fundamental building blocks of classical architecture.

The west facade and tower have a higher proportion of wall area (Cordova Cream and Cordova Shell limestone) to openings than the building's two wings, which house the architecture studios. The studios' east-west orientation, shallow depth, and large, operable windows take advantage of the prevailing breeze and provide ample

Goldsmith Hall

natural light. Between the wings is a superbly proportioned courtyard screened from the walk linking the West Mall and Sutton Hall by a loggia and an iron grille. The cartouches above the courtyard depict two fundamental systems of construction: post and beam (trabeated) and arch (arcuated).

Goldsmith Hall's general shape of block and wings framing a courtyard may be likened to that of a Renaissance palazzo, and its architects certainly had encyclopedic knowledge of many such buildings in Italy and Spain. Cret and his associates, in the spirit of Goodhue, found relevant principles of beauty, systems of organization, and modes of symbolic expression in the broad traditions of palazzo design and adapted them to their task of planning an architecture school in Texas. Working from these general principles to the specific, they variously drew on certain precedents, such as details of ornament, or departed from them, such as the steel-sash windows of the upper studio floors, in accordance with the character they had defined for the building.

Bill Booziotis took a similarly evolutionary approach in designing the addition, completed in 1988, which extended the west facade, created a new entrance facing Sutton Hall, and doubled the depth of the south wing. Booziotis made it possible for attentive observers to discern the addition through subtle devices such as the dark granite stripe and the abstractions of classical moldings. The most dramatic expression of the addition on the interior is the preservation of the original facade of the south wing, visible on the second and third floors and illuminated by a narrow skylight.

The renovation of the older portions of the building retained the two principal rooms at its center: the assembly room on the ground floor (transformed into an exhibition hall) and the library on the second floor (converted to studio space). The stencils on the concrete beams in the old library were painted in 1933 by Peter Allidi with recent graduates Harold "Bubi" Jessen and James Hammond and combine caricatures of UT faculty and administrators with images of pioneer Texas, famous buildings from the history of architecture, and icons of the machine age. They inspired the paintings of people and buildings significant in the 1980s on the beams above the south lobby on the first floor.

The renovation removed the last vestiges of the loge room in the basement (approximately in the location of today's woodshop) where, as part of the frequent design competitions organized by the Beaux-Arts Institute of Design, students sat isolated in small cubicles and worked out their initial schemes, known as *partis*. After registering their schemes with a supervisor, they would take them to their studios upstairs for elaboration. Two surviving traces of architectural pedagogy in the 1930s are the vaulted room with unadorned plaster walls in the tower that served as a studio for mural painting and the open trusses in the third-floor studios that were left unfinished and accessible so students could experiment with full-scale solutions for detailing ceilings.

8. Texas Union Building
Paul Cret, Consulting Architect; Robert Leon White, Architect, 1932; addition: Page Southerland Page and Mark Lemmon, Consulting Architects; Goleman & Rolfe, Associate Architect, 1958; renovation: Jessen & Associates, 1974

In the decade following World War I, the college union movement spread widely on American campuses. Particularly popular at state institutions, including the universities of Michigan, Wisconsin, Iowa, and Kansas, it addressed the need of the larger, increasingly heterogeneous populations of students, faculty, and alumni for

Texas Union Building

facilities where the university community could gather for fellowship, edification, and recreation. In 1922, a group of UT students organized a campaign to build a union dedicated to those from the university who had served in the war, but this effort was not successful. The new stadium assumed that memorial function, and plans for a student union went dormant until 1927, when Thomas Watt Gregory, president of the Ex-Students' Association (now the Texas Exes) began marshaling support for what became known as the Union Project. Under Gregory's leadership, the Exes took the lead raising funds for a Texas Union and three other buildings devoted to improving student life: Gregory Gymnasium, Anna Hiss Gymnasium, and Hogg Auditorium. University Supervising Architect Robert Leon White prepared the initial studies for the union building in 1929 and then worked in concert with Paul Cret, who became the university's Consulting Architect the following year.

The union has an L-shaped plan with the long wing along Guadalupe Street and the short wing on the West Mall. A tower at the intersection of the wings pairs with the tower on Goldsmith Hall to mark the entrance to the mall from the street. The reinforced-concrete skeleton (steel for the ballroom) is clad with irregularly coursed Cordova Shell limestone framed by Cordova Cream limestone. The two types of stone, asymmetrical massing, and complex fenestration patterns create a picturesque effect disciplined by the uniform color, the continuity of string courses, and the broad, overhanging eaves.

Cret and White designated most of the ground floor for dining rooms (the main room was the Commons) oriented toward the east-facing courtyard, which served as the primary entrance. The character of the original courtyard facade was less institutional than what we see today and invoked the *cortile* of a vaguely Spanish colonial residence.

The architects elaborated this imagery in the more formal public rooms on the second floor. From the grand entrance through the tower on the West Mall, a staircase leads to an interior cortile lit by a large skylight and surrounded by a wooden balcony adorned by portrait medallions of presidents of the university to 1933. They are the work of the Swiss woodcarver, Peter Heinrich Mansbendel, who also carved the images of the Texas frontier on the chest and the record player cabinet set along the walls. The cortile provides a point of orientation from which visitors disperse to the surrounding meeting rooms, offices of student organizations, and, above all, the grand ballroom.

Clues to the building's communal purpose appear in the reliefs along the west and south facades. Those on the west portray, from left to right, the totems of the School of Law (a creature known as Peregrinus), the College of Arts & Sciences (the Greek god Hermes), and the College of Engineering (Alexander Frederick Claire, or "Alec"). On the south facade a longhorn steer representing Bevo, the university's mascot since 1916, marks the entrance to the former snack bar, now the Cactus Cafe. Above the main entrance is the university seal, and to the right, above the original entrance to the Commons, another longhorn presides over symbols of learning. The three other entrances date from the renovation of the mid-1970s. Their sculpted panels symbolize the activities to be found within the Union.

The addition of 1960 on the north side of the building more than doubled its size with expanded food service areas, a movie theater, and recreational facilities that included a bowling alley. Although the new exterior cladding continued the limestone of the original building, the interior projected a sharply modernist appearance with chrome, stainless steel, and highlights of bright orange, yellow, red, lavender, and blue. This look lost its allure in the mid-1970s and yielded to a treatment more sympathetic to the original finishes, which guide renovations today.

Through its architecture and iconography, the Union, like many of the buildings of the 1920s and 1930s, evokes a mythic history of Texas grounded in its origin as a Spanish colonial outpost and idealization of life on the frontier. A few steps to the north of the Union are three ancient oak trees that stand as direct reminders of the natural history that predates this story. Believed to be among the oldest trees on campus, they are the remnants of the small groves that once dotted the grassy hill that became the Forty Acres. Threatened by the planning of the Biology building in 1923, Dr. William J. Battle, the chairman of the faculty building committee, stepped in and rallied support to assure their preservation. They are now known as the Battle Oaks.

9. Peter T. Flawn Academic Center

Jessen, Jessen, Millhouse and Greeven, Consulting Architect; George L. Dahl, Associate Architect, 1960

Originally called the Undergraduate Library and Academic Center, this pivotal campus landmark was renamed for an equally pivotal administrative figure,

Peter T. Flawn, in 1985. Flawn served as university president from 1979 to 1985, during which time he used the celebration of the university's centennial as an occasion to significantly boost both academic standards and fundraising capabilities.

The Flawn Center was conceived by another distinguished UT administrator, Harry Huntt Ransom. He considered Main Building's closed-stack library an architectural curiosity that was daunting to younger students. He modeled his new vision for an undergraduate library on the Lamont Library (1949) at Harvard University, which mixed, for the first time, open-stack access to books, enhanced audiovisual capabilities, exposure to special collections, and even a poetry reading room. Alcove seating and comfortable armchairs encouraged the idea of the library as a social space for informal interactions. Ransom imagined his library at UT accommodating "discussion groups among faculty and students in the company of books." Consistent with his passion for collecting, he envisioned a full floor of the library dedicated to an academic center with historic and special collections. Undergraduates would be able to browse art and precious manuscripts displayed along the wide hallways. Throughout the building, art, music, books, artifacts, history, and contemporary discourse would interact in a new way.

Ransom's architects designed a building faithful to his programmatic vision, yet offering flexibility, a hallmark of progressive design in the 1960s. There was a large, glass-enclosed exhibition foyer on the ground floor, books appropriate to undergraduates in open stacks on the second and third floors, and a rich assortment of displays and special collections on the top floor. The fourth floor, recently converted to office space, originally was organized around an open court, which, along with a generous terrace at the southeast corner, provided places for art, reading, and conversation outdoors. The central court and the wide galleries surrounding it contained works of art and cases displaying literary manuscripts that provided students with a taste of the special collections housed in surrounding rooms.

Peter T. Flawn Academic Center

The initial reaction to the innovative new facility was very positive. Patronage by its target audience, undergraduates, exceeded expectations, with more than seven thousand students passing through its doors each day. University library circulation increased by more than sixteen percent in the first year of operation and had nearly doubled by the end of the second year.

Changing patterns of undergraduate library use over the

years resulted in the removal of the book collection in 2005 and conversion of much of the building into a computing center. The flexibility built into the initial scheme greatly facilitated these drastic changes. Though the original role of the foyer as an exhibition space was short-lived, the space continues to be heavily used for informal study, group meetings, and even early voting. Its activities sometimes spill out to the generous terrazzo terraces to the east, south, and west. These active outdoor extensions, in turn, greatly enrich the life of the adjacent West Mall and Union courtyard.

In counterpoint to the generic modernity of its open plan and liberal use of glass and aluminum, Flawn Center's cladding of Cordova Cream and Cordova Shell limestone locate the building firmly on the UT campus. Its tripartite composition, with a base made of glass and black granite, a more neutral mid-section, and an ornate cap tie it to earlier buildings. Its top floor (once recessed, now filled in with glass) still carries an allusion to the Spanish belvederes that inspired the crowns of Mary E. Gearing Hall, the Texas Union, and Goldsmith Hall. The broad coffered soffits repeat a motif characteristic of many of the earlier structures on the Forty Acres.

Something of a 1960s period piece in composite, the Flawn Center has had its share of detractors over time. Its cast-stone solar screens on the second and third floors (a common mid-twentieth-century motif inspired by the work of Edward Durrell Stone) have sometimes seemed friendlier to roosting pigeons than to the human inhabitants within. Its relentless interior grid of acoustical tiles and fluorescent lights has sometimes been seen as an unfortunate dominance of technical function over warmth and human comfort. These drawbacks led to a lack of appreciation for the building's positive qualities that has resulted in many small desecrations of some of its best features over time.

10. Hogg Memorial Auditorium
Paul Cret, Consulting Architect; Robert Leon White, Architect, 1932

When building safety issues mandated the closure of the auditorium in Old Main in 1916, the university was without a large hall for assemblies, theatrical performances, and concerts. For such occasions it became necessary to rent space off campus, sometimes in the commercial theaters downtown. After a decade of such improvisation, the Ex-Students' Association made the construction of a new auditorium the final part of the Union Plan. Acting upon the Exes' recommendation, the Board of Regents dedicated the building to Governor James Stephen Hogg and his son, William Clifford Hogg, a former regent who had left the bulk of his estate to the university.

The auditorium's east-facing orientation is the result of compromise. Paul Cret placed the building on the north side of the Texas Union's courtyard, aligned with

Hogg Memorial Auditorium

an axis extending southward across the West Mall and down the hill to Sutton Hall. Although the Woman's Building (1903) was still standing in 1931, he anticipated its removal and the widening of the Union courtyard to correspond with the dimensions of the auditorium. The construction of the Peter T. Flawn Academic Center in 1963 obscured this relationship, but Cret's intention accounts for the projecting bay on the south facade auditorium (matched on the north) articulated by pilasters framing three large windows. The gesture is purely scenographic. Persons drawn to it in hopes of finding the entrance to the building must walk around to the east facade. This orientation allows a conventional sequence of lobby, auditorium, and stage; cross ventilation aligned with the prevailing breeze; entry without passing through the Union courtyard; and provision of a driveway; but it is awkward in terms of the arrangement of buildings and landscape in the area north of the Tower. An unrealized part of Cret's site plan was a small theater that was to have had a stage abutting the back of the auditorium and a public entrance on Guadalupe Street.

Apart from the finials at the corners of the east facade, the auditorium lacks the varied massing, fenestration, and ornamental details that lend a picturesque quality to the Union and Goldsmith Hall. The overall character is of a formal, stark neoclassicism.

The outer lobby is notable for the survival of most of its original tile, plaster, and wood finishes. Of particular significance are the geometric and floriated tile patterns that are echoed on a larger scale in the auditorium as grilles framing the proscenium. The auditorium seats slightly more than 1,300 persons on the ground floor and balcony. Missing today are the spots of color originally provided by a jade stage curtain and burnt orange draperies that covered the windows and doors. The stage and its equipment were state of the art at the time of completion and provided the university with a worthy venue for concert and theater tours and student productions.

11. Biological Laboratories
Herbert M. Greene, LaRoche and Dahl, 1925

Originally called the Biology Building, the general location and character of this first building completed on campus by Herbert M. Greene had been indicated in the master plan James M. White prepared for the university in 1923. The building's design looks to Gilbert's Sutton Hall (1918), its immediate predecessor. Like Sutton, it is a long, thin rectangle in plan with its long sides facing north and south and a double-loaded corridor down the center. It is basically a three-story volume with a basement, with the first floor faced in tooled Lueders limestone and the upper two stories faced in a brownish brick blend. Paired wooden brackets support the deep overhang of a hipped red tile roof. Terra-cotta ornament animates and adds color in trim around selected doors and windows.

One significant challenge, however, that required Greene's ingenuity in adapting the Sutton Hall formula, was the ten-foot slope descending along the length of the building from west to east. Greene took advantage of the situation to transform what would otherwise be just a basement level at the east end into a well-lit habitable floor. In so doing he gave the lower level a strong architectural expression by introducing horizontal bands of stone with deeply recessed reveals that rise out of the sloping ground to create a solid foothold on which the classically composed building rests.

Greene also utilized the full volume of the building more completely than Gilbert had done at Sutton by adding a habitable floor in the space of the entablature and roof. Where Gilbert had placed small ventilators flanked by ornamental griffins between the roof brackets, Greene inserted commodious windows allowing generous (though eccentrically placed) sources of light and views for rooms inside. The very economical combination of well-lit basement and attic space created a functional five-story building in the same general envelope that had been a three-story building in the case of Sutton.

A priority for economy was evident throughout the building. The interiors were plain, even austere. Terra-cotta use was greatly simplified with salmon-colored plain square tiles and blue accents replacing the more elaborate articulation of Sutton in many places. An exception is the primary entrance. Oriented away from the Forty Acres and facing 24th Street, this portal contains Ionic columns, griffins, and other classical motifs also common to Sutton Hall. But there is some distinctly new iconography here as well—abstracted cow skulls, lone stars, and lots of cacti.

Biological Laboratories

Elsewhere on the building, emblems of flora and fauna appropriate for a biology building are also regionalized to include bluebonnets and oak branches, familiar symbols of the still-rural state in the 1920s.

12. Mary E. Gearing Hall

Paul Cret, Consulting Architect; Herbert M. Greene, LaRoche and Dahl, Architect, 1932

Known as the Home Economics Building until 1976, Mary E. Gearing Hall was renamed for the first woman to hold the ranks of professor and department chair at the University of Texas. Professor Gearing was recruited in 1912 to begin a home economics program for the university and served as its leader for thirty-one years. The building was designed to accommodate instruction in nutrition, food economics, textiles, and child development.

Strategically located between the Forty Acres and the women's campus, the design for this academic building, also primarily for women, was significantly site-driven. Its location served as a differentiator and a gateway between two important campus districts and also sat squarely on the grand axis that ran from the Capitol, along the South Mall, through the Main Building and the Tower, and continued, in altered form, to the north.

Mary E. Gearing Hall

One of Cret's boldest moves in the master development plan that he was preparing as he designed his first campus buildings was to interrupt the North Mall with what would become Gearing Hall. This critical building was to face north to a well-defined space of identical width and even greater length compared to the South Mall. Between it and the Main Building would be a soft, green court. Thus, Cret envisioned the sequence of spaces along the main axis of the campus changing from the highly symmetrical and urbane ensemble south of the Main Building to a more relaxed, intimate, and informal arrangement on the north.

Gearing Hall is a near-perfect expression of those master plan intentions at an architectural scale. The varied roof profiles, with a large hipped volume on the central wing, flat roofs on the lower wings, and two picturesque towers gives the composition an informal character, as if it had been built in stages over time. The little patio at the center of the building's U-shaped composition would have reinforced the more intimate character of the north side of the campus and presented an appropriate introduction for those entering the building as the gateway to the women's campus.

Though the vaguely Spanish flavor of earlier campus buildings was still clearly evident, Cret noted in his "Report" of 1933 that "old stone houses in Austin" made of rough, almost crude rubble were "another source of inspiration." He imagined a simpler, more rustic feeling than was present in the buildings designed by Gilbert and Greene. The construction drawings indicate that highly textured, irregular rubble was to be used for the walls, complementing the wood brackets and balcony rails in the upper portion of the building and the heavy timber beams, rafters, and decking of the loggia around the courtyard. For reasons of cost, random ashlar stone was used instead, diminishing the rustic effect.

Window patterns in Gearing Hall also contribute to its less formal architectural character. Especially on the four-story portion, fenestration is loosely composed and varies from floor to floor. Lower floors have punched rectangular windows that do not quite stack. The top floor, under the eaves, is treated as if it were a closed-in gallery reminiscent of Moorish belvederes.

But it is in the fifteen-foot-deep loggia around the courtyard that one really feels the romantic intimacy of this building that was so different from its campus predecessors. The deep shadows that contrast so strongly with the hot southern sun, the quiet trickle of the central fountain, the frank expression of heavy wood framing in ceilings and window lintels, and the simple, unarticulated stone piers all speak to a deep, rich heritage that is captured here without resorting to mimicry or replication.

Although the interior has undergone changes, traces of Mary Gearing's intention to use the building as a pedagogical demonstration of various finishes and furnishings remain. Of particular note is the suite of rooms on the third floor presenting a parlor and dining room commemorating the life of women during the Republic of Texas.

13. T. S. Painter Hall

Paul Cret, Consulting Architect; Herbert M. Greene, LaRoche and Dahl, Architect, 1932; addition: Mark Lemmon, Consulting Architect; Fehr and Granger, Associate Architect, 1958

Known originally as the Physics Building, Painter Hall was renamed in 1969 for Theophilus Shickel Painter, a physics professor who worked at the university for fifty-three years and served as its thirteenth president from 1946 to 1952. It was located on the so-called "Science Row" between the Biological Laboratories to the west and the Chemistry Building (now Welch Hall) to the east. These three buildings formed a strong northern border for the Forty Acres, with their primary entrances on 24th Street. Painter, paired with the Biological Laboratories, framed the axis extending from the Main Building to Gearing Hall across the street. This was a critical site for accomplishing the campus space-making goals Paul Cret outlined in his Development Plan of 1933.

T. S. Painter Hall

Although Painter was successful in terms of urban design, it was one of the least resolved and least architecturally sophisticated of Cret's buildings on the campus. From its inception, Painter was a hodgepodge of dissimilar elements. At its core is a simple four-story rectangular volume with a double-loaded corridor down the center and a hipped red-tile roof, similar to the Biological Laboratories, Sutton Hall, or Waggener Hall. There is a familiar "bookends" treatment on the north facade with vertically articulated volumes to the east and west framing an elaborate entry portal at the center. To the west, however, the end volume extends to a greater height, breaking the line of the roof to form a tower that framed the north axis from the Main Building. A short, flat-roofed wing extends south from the rectangular volume at the east end, further complicating the building's massing. A twenty-foot-tall copper dome housing a telescope is perched precariously on the roof in the very center of the composition.

The scale, composition, and proportion of the tower at the west end offer a startling contrast to the lower rectangular volume. Graceful arched windows on three sides of the top floor of the tower create a lovely ensemble and signal the presence of the physics library within. A tall band of brick above these windows lends a monumental scale to the tower, matched by a two-story stone base at the bottom. On its own, the tower volume is quite handsome, but as a part of the larger composition, it seems awkward and out of place.

Two of the interior spaces were memorable architecturally. The physics library on the top floor was distinguished by its high ceilings, generous daylight (though most of it was from the west) and seven beautiful arched windows. After extensive remodeling, this space is, unfortunately, almost unrecognizable today. Below the library, Cret placed a lecture hall seating 200 people, which is still one of the best large classrooms on campus.

In 1959, the flat-roofed south wing of the building was extended in a manner very similar to the expansion of the footprint indicated on Cret's Development Plan of 1933. The new extension replicates the detail of the original building's exterior in such a way that the addition is indistinguishable at first glance. The interior treatment of the addition is, however, quite different, with glazed block corridors that clearly mark a different era.

14. Dorothy L. Gebauer Building
Coughlin and Ayres, 1904; renovations: Cotera, Kolar, Negrete, 2000

Originally built for the departments of Civil, Mining, and Electrical Engineering and called the Engineering Building, this storied structure became the Journalism Building from 1932 to 1952, the Speech Building from 1952 to 1976, and the Student Services Building from 1976 to 1984. At that point it was renamed for Dorothy H. Gebauer, a longtime dean of women. It continued to be used for student services until it was condemned for structural problems in 1992.

The Gebauer Building has earned its position as the oldest structure on the campus built for university purposes only after many trials. It was slated for demolition as early as 1933, and Cret designed Inner Campus Drive and the Will C. Hogg Building cheek-to-jowl beside it with the assumption it would be razed, but it never was. Its condemnation in 1992 almost assured its demise, until Professor Dan Leary in the School of Architecture led the charge to save it. That rescue provoked a thorough reconstruction and renovation in 2000 that prepared it to become the administrative offices for the College of Liberal Arts, its current use.

The renovation kept the exterior of the building true to its original appearance, while adding greater accessibility for the mobility impaired, and a new steel fire escape on the east side. The interior has been returned to a general look of the period of its turn-of-the-century construction, but its layout was altered to accommodate administrative functions.

Dorothy L. Gebauer Building

An early work of San Antonio architect Atlee B. Ayres (who would become one of the leading architects in Texas of his generation), the building reflects the Beaux-Arts training of its architect, who had not yet found the preference for Mediterranean-style building that would characterize much of his later career.

Gebauer's odd stylistic character—its yellow brick, for example, that matched Old Main but appears out of place today—and its awkward relationship to the buildings, grade changes, and roads around it all make it a bit of a misfit—a function of its charmed history. Much lore is attached to its long, eclectic history—from engineering students tinkering with turbines in the basement, to the U.S. Weather Bureau monitoring temperatures in a weather station set up on its flat roof, to news giants such as Walter Cronkite, Liz Carpenter, and Liz Smith cutting their teeth by churning out stories for the campus newspaper during its years as the Journalism Building.

15. Robert A. Welch Hall

Herbert M. Greene, LaRoche and Dahl, 1929; west wing addition: Page Southerland Page, Consulting Architect, Goleman & Rolfe, Associate Architect, 1961; east wing addition: Wyatt C. Hedrick, 1974; renovation: Graeber, Simmons & Cowan, 1979

After a fire in 1926 burned down the Chemical Laboratory (built by Burt McDonald, 1892), located near the present turtle pond, the university commissioned Herbert M. Greene to design a larger, better-equipped facility at the corner of 24th Street and Speedway in alignment with the Biological Laboratories. The new Chemistry Building provided classrooms and laboratories accommodating 1,280 students as well as a library, faculty offices, and workshops. It was the largest academic building on campus after Old Main and considerably more sophisticated in terms of its specialized equipment for ventilation and the supply of distilled water, gas, and other laboratory materials.

Robert A. Welch Hall

The facades echo the composition of the Biological Laboratories and employ the same brick and Lueders limestone, but they depart from the model by introducing steel casement windows and reducing the use of terra-cotta to a few details: the roll molding along the sills of the upper windows, geometric ornament beneath the eaves, and panels bearing the university seal, chemical symbols, and the names of famous chemists. Greene reserved the most dramatic gesture for the limestone retablo portal that frames the main entrance. This is the first expression of this monumental feature of Spanish colonial architecture on campus and established a theme upon which Paul Cret would compose numerous variations.

In plan, the original building resembles the letter E with the wings facing south. The lower floor of the center wing contains the main lecture hall, which still retains its beamed ceiling elaborately painted with symbols of Texas and alchemy. The chemistry library was above, and though it has been relocated beneath the courtyard, the original doors remain, with panels of stained glass representing the university seal and chemical apparatuses.

The 1961 addition doubled the length of the westernmost wing but provided only a short-term fix for the heavy demands on the building by ever-increasing student enrollment and expanded faculty research activity. Thirteen years later, the building was more than doubled in size by the construction of wings extending along Speedway to the East Mall and from Speedway to the 1961 addition. A two-level courtyard faces the south facade of the original building, and a complex sequence of ramps, stairs, and terraces leads to the street-sized interior corridor serving the building's largest lecture halls and classrooms. Welch Hall honors Robert Alonzo Welch, a Houston businessman whose philanthropic interests include chemical research and education.

16. Will C. Hogg Building

Paul Cret, Consulting Architect; Herbert M. Greene, LaRoche and Dahl, Architect, 1932

For the Hogg Building, Paul Cret employed the fundamental characteristics of the palazzo-inspired building format introduced by Cass Gilbert and elaborated by Herbert M. Greene. He showed great respect for Garrison Hall in particular, situated just to the south, which he mirrored in height, length, and the way in which he negotiated the steeply sloped site.

In terms of fenestration, smaller scale facade treatment, and detail, however, Cret made significant departures from the work of his predecessors. He established literal classical orders that are not present in the work of Gilbert or Greene by creating thirty-two, two-story brick pilasters with terra-cotta Ionic capitals that dominate all four facades. They rest on a one-story stone base on the west end that turns into a

Will C. Hogg Building

two-story stone base on the other three sides because of the terraced slope. The brick is lighter and yellower than that used by Gilbert and Greene and the limestone is Cordova Cream rather than the Lueders that was preferred in the base of earlier buildings. The stone is smooth-cut but laid in a random ashlar pattern, another departure. The quoins on the corners of the base, however, reiterate the strong horizontal bands and deep recesses Greene had used in Garrison and elsewhere.

Cret introduced a new material, gray slate, between the windows of the top two floors to create a dark vertical slot between the double-order of the pilasters. Most of the iconography of the building is concentrated in a horizontal frieze constituting a transition between the stone base and the two-story pierced brick volume above. The frieze extends around the entire building and indicates clearly the original function of Hogg as the home for the Geology Department. The continuous band alternates long thin panels representing fossils of Central Texas with squarish panels depicting fish, crystals, reptiles, an insect, a crab, and a mastodon, among various other creatures. The buff colored panels are actually terra-cotta tiles manufactured by a firm of sculptors in Denver, under the direction of faculty members in the Geology Department.

The building is named for Will C. Hogg, a lawyer and benefactor to the university and the son of Texas Governor James Stephen Hogg. The younger Hogg served on the Board of Regents and as president of the Texas Exes in the early twentieth century.

17. Computation Center

Jessen, Jessen, Millhouse and Greeven, Consulting Architect;
Fehr and Granger, Associate Architect, completed 1961

It must have seemed like a clever idea at the time. A new facility was needed for emerging computation devices, which by today's standards were enormous. The Computation Center needed to be centrally located on a campus that was considered pretty much built out at its core. To create a space for the new building near the heart of campus, the paved terrace to the east of the Main Building was extended an additional 82 feet and the 15,000-square-foot building was tucked under it. The east face and portions of the north faces are visible as the building protrudes out of the sloping site.

Computation Center

Three problems emerged. First, as computer science became a major field of study and computing permeated all facets of academic life, the building was quickly much too small; because of its land-locked location, there was no room for expansion. Second, the building was essentially all basement space; most rooms were poorly lit and had no views. Third, the extension obstructed an important axis between the entry of Garrison Hall to the south and the entry to the Will C. Hogg Building to the north. Those two entries became far less accessible, and their address on the newly extended East Mall became insignificant.

18. Waggener Hall

Herbert M. Greene, LaRoche and Dahl, 1931

Construction on Waggener Hall, the last building Herbert M. Greene completed as University Architect, had not yet begun when Paul Cret was hired to create a new development plan for the university in 1930. It marked the end of an era during which Greene had designed twelve landmark buildings that shaped the campus significantly and would serve the university exceedingly well for decades to come.

Waggener Hall

As with the Biological Laboratories, Garrison Hall, and Welch Hall, Greene utilized the palazzo as a starting point for Waggener. The fact that the building was to be long and thin and parallel to the slope of the site meant he did not have to resolve the conflict between a flat-site building format and the sloping terrain of the Forty Acres as he had elsewhere. But the program did require more functional space than a three-story building like Sutton Hall could accommodate on this limited site. In response, Greene modified the general format to create five floors—a ground floor faced in Lueders limestone, three floors above faced in a brown/tan/ochre brick blend, and a top floor worked into the entablature.

Waggener Hall differs from the earliest of the palazzo-format buildings because its ground floor does not have arched windows and is faced with horizontal bands of stone with recessed joints. Windows are steel sash rather than wood, and terra-cotta is employed only in occasional ornamental panels. Waggener has cleaner lines and crisper detail than any of the other Greene buildings. Its geometry is more prominent and its ornament more spare.

Where ornament does occur, it has a very clear message. Waggener Hall's iconography is dedicated to depictions of Texas commerce (fitting for a building that originally housed business administration). Medallions around the top of the building portray the foundations of the Texas economy at the time of the building's construction. The twenty panels depict the mineral and agricultural basis of the state's industry through images of oil derricks, livestock, crops, cotton bolls, and a pine tree to represent timber. Like Garrison Hall just to the west, Waggener Hall is firmly rooted in Texas.

The building was named for Leslie Waggener, one of the first professors hired when UT opened its doors in 1883. He served as chairman of the faculty from 1884 to 1894 and became the first president of the university when the post was established in 1895.

19. McCombs School of Business

Page Southerland Page, 1959; addition and renovation: Graeber, Simmons & Cowan, Inc. with R. Max Brooks FAIA, Project Architect, 1983

When the new home of the College of Business Administration was opened in 1962, it was designated the B. E. B. (Business-Economics Building) which students quickly interpreted as an acronym for "Big Enormous Building." It was, indeed, the largest classroom building on the campus and the seven-story north block was the tallest on campus after the Main Building.

The B. E. B. was also the first modern building to be built on the Forty Acres—not only in its clean, geometric volumes and lines, but also in its planning and functional operation. The complex was composed of three distinct volumes provoked by separate programmatic needs. A five-story classroom building with a basement was organized around an open central courtyard. Its plan arrangement was clear, logical, and analytical, driven by program, function, technical performance, and flexibility in good modern fashion.

The second volume of the complex was a compact, efficient office building for faculty and staff containing 221 offices arranged with executive spaces oriented to the outside and administrative spaces contained in a core. Most windows in this volume faced north and south for preferred solar orientation. The third volume provided the main entry to the complex from the west as well as primary horizontal circulation for the complex

McCombs School of Business

via bridges that connected the classroom building and the office building. It also contained escalators for vertical circulation—the first to appear on campus. The long east and west faces of this volume were protected from the Texas sun by perforated screens that admitted some daylight, but reduced heat gain.

The modernism of the B. E. B. was well-received in the progressive 1960s. In 1969, the magazine of the Texas Exes, *Alcalde*, admired "this strikingly modern building standing incongruously next to one of the oldest campus eyesores, Pearce Hall." The article further credited "the innovative look of the new place" with provoking progressive changes in the business curriculum that emphasized modern "systems, models, and solutions."

Even though its flat roofs, structural clarity and crisp detail all made the B. E. B. seem refreshingly modern at the time, the design of the complex contained many gestures that tied it back to previous campus buildings as well. Its dominant material was a brick blend that was a slightly toned-down reflection of the brick used in Waggener Hall and Gregory Gymnasium to the north and east. Its first-floor base was made of the familiar Cordova Cream limestone and Texas Pink granite, laid in horizontal bands with deep reveals similar to the base of Waggener. The classroom portion of the complex had deep overhangs with coffered soffits like most of the older buildings on campus, and the top floor was treated as a sort of belvedere with dark red clay tile screens recalling the Moorish quality Cret gave to several of his buildings. (The screens were removed and the windows replaced on the top floor in 2008 removing all vestiges of this motif.)

The office portion of the complex featured fifty ceramic reliefs at the top of the north, west, and south facades with abstract designs in two shades of blue, gold, black, and taupe. Created by Paul Peter Hatgil, who taught in the Art Department from 1951 to 1985, these custom-made panels recall the polychrome terra-cotta work on many of the older campus buildings.

The functional flexibility built into the B. E. B. has been fully utilized during its decades of service. The School of Business has seen more enrollment fluctuations and more new initiatives than most other departments, and the building has had to change with them. In the classroom portion of the complex, only the fourth floor has an arrangement of spaces similar to the original building. Other floors have accommodated large, open computer labs, generous spaces for social interaction and many suites for specific program needs.

In the early 1970s the Graduate School of Business was grafted onto the west face of the complex. In 1983, the expansion of enrollment in the school to almost ten thousand students provoked a very extensive renovation. The original circulation volume of the complex was radically altered to provide a "Hall of Honor" on the ground floor and an events space above, and to create a major new entry faced in travertine and dark glass on the east side of the building. The courtyard was closed in to accommodate a central lounge space next to a new cafe.

Graduate School of Business

In honor of his record-breaking fifty-million-dollar gift to the School of Business in 2000, the complex was renamed for Red McCombs, a San Antonio businessman who had attended UT business and law schools in the early 1950s.

20. Graduate School of Business
Kenneth Bentsen & Associates, 1976; renovation: Graeber, Simmons & Cowan, Inc. with R. Max Brooks FAIA, Project Architect, 1983

Prompted by a 400 percent increase in graduate business enrollment over a decade, this eccentric structure was grafted onto the west side of the McCombs School of Business. Pearce Hall (Atlee B. Ayres, architect, 1908) was demolished to make way for it, but a valiant effort was made to save nine mature live oak trees that had graced the north lawn of the old home for the Law School. As a means of dodging the trees and also creating a new plaza facing Perry-Castañeda Library, the plan of the Graduate School of Business took the unusual form of a parallelogram. The exterior is clad in large areas of darkly tinted glass alternating with even larger areas of travertine. In shape, scale, materials, and general appearance, the structure contrasts starkly with both the adjoining building and the immediate context around it.

It offers a very different character from previous campus environments on the interior as well. Newspaper articles at the time it opened noted its "sophisticated veneer" and compared it to "the corporate headquarters of an IBM or U.S. Steel." They said it "almost breathes the spirit of a thriving business." Wide passages were meant to create special opportunities for informal gathering and discussion and classrooms with horseshoe-shaped seating were intended to encourage intimacy and interaction.

21. Littlefield Fountain

Pompeo Coppini, Sculptor; Paul Cret, Consulting Architect, dedicated 1933

The imposing bronze figures, cascading water, and axial alignment with the Tower make Littlefield Fountain one of the most photographed sites on campus, but once they have taken the picture, few people linger to consider its meaning. An inventory of its components reveals it to be a World War I monument. Three sea horses, two ridden by Tritons, pull a ship bearing Columbia, who holds the torch of liberty and a palm frond signifying peace; she is accompanied by a muscular soldier and sailor. The dates inscribed on the prow mark American's entry in the conflict and Armistice Day. A bronze plaque on the north side of the monument lists the names of the ninety-seven alumni who died in the service of their country, and the Latin text carved in stone above quotes the Roman philosopher, Cicero, on the universal honor accorded to patriotism. The 2007 restoration of the fountain underwritten by Steve and Rita Millwee expanded its role as a memorial to include all who have served in the U.S. armed forces.

Commemoration of the War to End All Wars was not the only objective of the benefactor for whom the fountain is named. In 1914, university benefactor and Confederate veteran George Washington Littlefield approached Pompeo Coppini about creating a monument to the Confederacy on campus that would complement the sculptor's 1903 bronze Memorial to the Confederate Dead on the state's Capitol grounds. Littlefield's vision exceeded what he was prepared to spend, but five years later he again approached Coppini with a larger budget. His persistence was fueled in part by concern that the university would accept the offer of his rival, George Washington Brackenridge, to relocate the campus to the tract Brackenridge had donated along the shore of Lady Bird Lake. The memorial gateway project was part of the strategy Littlefield devised to obligate the university to remain on the Forty Acres.

Littlefield Fountain

At Coppini's suggestion, Littlefield revised the theme of the memorial to become a monument of reconciliation portraying World War I as the catalyst that inspired Americans to put aside differences lingering from the Civil War and unite in carrying the torch of liberty to the Old World. In addition to Columbia's ship, Coppini's design for the monument included two pylons serving as backdrops for bronze statues of the president of the Confederacy, Jefferson Davis, and the president who led the United States in World War I, Woodrow Wilson. They were to be flanked by statues of four figures selected by Littlefield: Confederate General Robert E. Lee; John H. Reagan, prominent Texas politician from the early days of statehood and Confederate postmaster; Albert Sidney Johnston, officer in the armies of the Republic of Texas, the United States, and the Confederacy, killed at the battle of Shiloh; and James Stephen Hogg, the first native-born governor of Texas and an ardent supporter of the university and public education. The monument's vision of reconciliation had a distinctly southern perspective, including the choice of Woodrow Wilson, also a southerner, as the representative of national leadership.

Littlefield died in 1920, but Coppini proceeded with the commission and had nearly completed it when Paul Cret arrived on the scene as Consulting Architect a decade later. Cret found the composition of the monument incompatible with his design for the South Mall. He felt it was out of scale and a distraction to the long vista he planned from 21st Street to Main Building. Accordingly, he redesigned the water basins, placed the statues of Lee, Reagan, Johnston, and Hogg along the edges of the mall, and erected the statues of Davis and Wilson on the terrace facing Main Building. The dispersal of the statues eviscerated Coppini's conception and is the cause of much of today's confusion about their purpose. Separated from their intended context, however contrived it might have been, the statues are all too easily seen as separate memorials rather than the product of a singular vision. The presence of the statue of George Washington further confuses interpretation because while it, too, is by Coppini, it was a gift of the Daughters of the American Revolution in 1955 and has nothing to do with Littlefield's gateway.

22. Homer Rainey Hall

Paul Cret, Consulting Architect and George Dahl of LaRoche, Dahl & Associates, Associate Architects, 1942

In 1938, the newly founded College of Fine Arts greeted its first class of 129 students with 10 faculty members and no permanent facilities for instruction. The lack of bricks and mortar was but a temporary condition in the minds of the college's energetic young dean, E. William Doty, university president Homer Price Rainey, and the influential chair of the faculty building committee, William J. Battle, who together envisioned a fine arts complex arising in the southwest quadrant of the Forty Acres.

Homer Rainey Hall

One of the challenges in planning the proposed fine arts complex (and a reason why the site soon proved unsuitable for the College of Fine Arts) was adapting the guidelines of Paul Cret's master plan to the technical requirements of buildings housing the making and presentation of art, music, and theater. Rainey Hall, which was to house the department of music, a concert hall, and the administrative office of the college, required a prominent location in this setting and as much separation as possible from the traffic noise of Guadalupe Street. These considerations account for its placement at the corner of the South Mall and the presence of three imposing entrances facing the mall, 21st Street, and the plaza. As the first of the South Mall buildings to be realized, its features set a precedent for the five classroom buildings that would complete the ensemble.

Rainey Hall presents itself as a two-story block with rusticated Cordova Shell limestone walls framed by ashlar Cordova Cream limestone quoins and a pronounced entablature. Frontispieces and balconies mark the entrances. The concert hall occupies a low block to the north, flanked along the east by a loggia accessible from the auditorium and the South Mall. The restrained ornamentation offers no indication of the building's purpose as the home of the music department, but a clue to that effect can be seen outside the left entrance of the loggia where the one surviving boot-scraper is adorned with eighth notes.

The generic classicism of the exterior belies the complexity of the building within, which at the time of completion in 1942 was one of the most sophisticated structures on campus due to the need for acoustic isolation of the building from its surroundings and of the practice rooms, offices, and performance spaces from each other. Rainey Hall was designed during a period of rapid innovation in the science of acoustics, and the university had guidance from an in-house expert in the field. C. Paul Boner, a professor of physics, collaborated with outside specialists, including C. C. Potwin, and the project architect, George Dahl, in specifying layout, materials, and construction. The building was among the first on campus to be fully air-conditioned, which allowed for an elaborate system of sound locks separating practice rooms and faculty studios and the insertion of a windowless floor of practice rooms at the level of the cornice. Acoustic considerations determined the thickness and positioning of the oak panels (some of which were lost in a 2009 renovation) lining the 500-seat concert hall, Jessen Auditorium, which contained a large, Aeolian-Skinner pipe organ (only the facade pipes remain in situ; since 2005, the organ has been housed in the sanctuary of St. Andrew's Episcopal Church in Amarillo).

Mezes Hall

Batts Hall

Appointed university president in 1939, Homer Price Rainey's time in office was marked by the challenges brought on by World War II and by assaults on academic freedom by members of the Board of Regents. They fired him in 1944 for obstructing their efforts to dismiss faculty they deemed politically unacceptable.

23. Benedict Hall
24. Mezes Hall
25. Batts Hall

Harbeson, Hough, Livingston and Larson, Consulting Architects;
Mark Lemmon, Consulting Architect; Staub and Rather, Associate
Architects, 1950; renovations and additions: 3D/International,
Inc., 2004

Designed by the same team and constructed at the same time, this three-in-one complex began its life as functionally separate buildings, each occupied by different academic units. Benedict Hall, home to the Mathematics Department, was separated from Mezes Hall, home to Philosophy and Psychology, by a 95-foot-wide court with a covered walkway at the east side. Mezes, in turn, was separated from Batts Hall, home to various foreign language departments, by a shallower court of the same width and a 480-seat auditorium that had its entry and lobby in Batts.

The joined-at-the-hip triplets all had the same footprint (55 feet wide by 150 feet long) as well as the same materials, fenestration pattern, and detail. They bore a

Benedict Hall

Parlin Hall   *Calhoun Hall*

striking resemblance to their sibling across the South Mall, Homer Rainey Hall, which had been completed nine years earlier. In fact, about the only distinguishing feature in the primary volumes of the newer buildings was the presence of fenestration in the top floor entablature. All three buildings had curiously anticlimactic entries from the gracious South Mall into fire stairs with glazed tile walls. There was a slightly grander entry on the south face of Benedict and on the north face of Batts.

Although a two-phase renovation of all three buildings (completed in 2007) radically reconfigured the interiors, aside from the replacement of operable steel-sash windows with slightly chunkier fixed aluminum units and the addition of a not-so-well-proportioned facade on the addition between Mezes and Benedict, the exteriors remain very much as they were in 1953 when the buildings were dedicated. Inside, however, both the arrangement of rooms and the finish materials are now quite different.

The buildings are named for three gentlemen of about the same age, all of whom played important roles in the development of the university. Judge Robert Lynn Batts taught in the Law School from 1893 to 1901, was Texas Exes president in 1890 and was chair of the Board of Regents in the early 1930s. Sidney Edward Mezes founded the Psychology Department in 1898 and served as UT's fifth president, between 1908 and 1914. Harry Yandell Benedict was president of Texas Exes in 1903 and 1907 and served as the university's tenth president from 1927 to 1937. It was during Benedict's tenure that the infamous shacks were removed from the campus and were replaced with twenty-one of the finest buildings the university has ever built. Each of the three buildings contains a bronze plaque featuring a profile portrait of its namesake. Charles Umlauf, a well-known sculptor on the Art Department faculty, designed the plaques.

26. Parlin Hall

Mark Lemmon, Consulting Architect; Broad and Nelson, Associate Architect, 1954

Known as the English Building until 1968, when it was renamed for Dr. H. T. Parlin, who held teaching appointments in the English Department from 1908 to 1951 and was Dean of Arts and Sciences from 1928 to 1950, the northwest anchor of the "six-pack" was the fifth in the sequence of buildings lining the South Mall to be completed. It borrows a great deal from its predecessors; the exterior of its main wing is almost a mirror image of Batts Hall, its neighbor directly across the mall.

27. Calhoun Hall

Brooks, Barr, Graeber and White, Consulting Architect; Pitts, Mebane, Phelps and White, Associate Architect, 1968

When Calhoun Hall finally filled in the "missing tooth" in the six-building ensemble lining the South Mall, it was a full thirty-five years after Paul Cret had conceived the group. Given its architectural character, it is hard to believe the building is a contemporary of Jester Center and was completed five years after Flawn Academic Center.

Calhoun Hall reflects essentially the same footprint as the other buildings in the "six-pack," slipping neatly between the ells of Homer Rainey Hall to the south and Parlin Hall to the north. The building also serves to define two nicely scaled courtyards in concert with those neighbors. Calhoun's massing, materials, and ornamentation were roughly borrowed from its brethren, though there is more variation from the norm here than in the other five buildings in the ensemble.

The most significant departure from the group is the insertion of arcades around the perimeter of the building on the ground floor. The segmented arches used in lower floor windows in the other buildings become the basis for a deep, shady space that provides outdoor entry points for a lecture hall, rest rooms, elevator lobby, and stairs to upper floors. The arcade also provides handy east/west access in this part of campus, providing a connection between the South Mall and the court in front of the Harry Ransom Center.

The building was named shortly after its completion for Dr. John W. Calhoun, professor of mathematics, the university's first Comptroller and acting President from 1937 to 1939.

WALK TWO: WOMEN'S CAMPUS, COMMUNICATIONS

From the beginning, The University of Texas at Austin has opened its doors to women as well as men. The University Catalogue of 1890 proudly noted, "In no respects are the young women considered as constituting a separate department of the University…and no distinction between them and the young men, either in discipline or instruction, is recognized." This egalitarian assertion proved bolder than the views of subsequent administrators, and by 1897 the Board of Regents described female students as "delicate and refined physical organisms [that] should be cared for," a point of view that must have raised an eyebrow or two among the women who had worked their way to the university from ranches and farms across Texas. In this spirit, the Regents proclaimed the urgent need for "a Woman's Building, wherein the young women may live on the campus, close to their work."[1]

Despite the stated urgency, the first on-campus residence for women was not completed until 1903, thirteen years after the construction of B. Hall, the men's dormitory. Designed by the San Antonio firm of Coughlin & Ayres, the Woman's Building stood on what is now the courtyard between the Texas Union and Hogg Auditorium, well apart from the boisterous inhabitants of B. Hall on the other side of Old Main. Unlike the bare-bones facilities of B. Hall, the Woman's Building featured a well-appointed parlor and dining room, an elevator, and the university's first gymnasium and pool. It served as a dormitory until 1940, when it was converted for academic use. Following a fire in 1959, it was demolished to make way for the Peter T. Flawn Academic Center.

The Woman's Building housed only eighty-five students. Other women in the first decades of the twentieth century found lodging in boarding houses and private dormitories, such as the Scottish Rite Dormitory, built by the Scottish Rite Masons in 1922. Designed by Herbert M. Greene just at the time the Board of Regents appointed him University Architect, it stands three blocks north of the Forty Acres on 27th Street between Whitis and University avenues. Facing All Saints' Chapel, it marked the edge of a neighborhood of stately homes. Its location was pivotal in the plans Greene and James M. White subsequently developed for what became known as the women's campus.

In 1921, the legislature allocated funds for the university to purchase property between 24th and 26th streets from Whitis Avenue to Waller Creek. A bequest from George Washington Littlefield made possible the construction of Littlefield Dormitory. Greene and White located it on 26th Street, aligned with the Scottish Rite Dormitory a block to the north. A block south and to the east on the axis of 25th Street, they planned a women's gymnasium (Anna Hiss Gymnasium, completed in 1931) and sports fields.

Greene and White's siting of Littlefield Dormitory and Anna Hiss Gymnasium provided the framework for the cross-axial arrangement of buildings that Paul Cret developed in his master plan a few years later. To the south of Littlefield Dormitory, he located residence halls separated by courtyards oriented toward the gymnasium.

The units were to be tied together along Whitis Avenue by arcades and another dormitory centered on 25th Street. North of 26th Street (now Dean Keeton Street), Cret reserved two parcels of land for future expansion. They became the sites for Kinsolving Dormitory and the Women's Cooperative Houses in the 1950s.

Cret maintained a degree of separation between the women's campus and the Forty Acres by locating the Home Economics Building (now Gearing Hall) directly on axis with the new Main Building on 24th Street. Behind it, University Avenue was laid out as an allée along the middle of three terraces that mediated the prominent slope toward Waller Creek. The dormitories occupied the first and highest terrace, and the gymnasium rested on the lowest.

Cret's plan was only partially realized by his construction of two dormitories, Carothers and Andrews halls. With Littlefield Dormitory, they frame a large, single courtyard known today as the Quad. The construction of Blanton Hall along University Avenue in 1955 isolated the Quad from the approach to Anna Hiss Gymnasium, which, today, has nearly disappeared among the science buildings erected between University Avenue and Speedway. Traces of the garden-like character Cret had intended for the women's campus can still be seen in the staircases and fragments of balustrades that mark the edges of the terraces.

Littlefield Home, Carriage House

28. Littlefield Home and Carriage House
James Wahrenberger, 1893

The Littlefield Home is the last of the gracious houses that once formed a residential neighborhood north of the Forty Acres. It was the home of George Washington Littlefield, one of the university's greatest benefactors at the turn of the twentieth century. Through his will, he funded Littlefield Dormitory and donated his home to the university.

Littlefield and his wife, Alice, selected James Wahrenberger as the architect for their house. Trained in Karlsruhe, Germany, and practicing in San Antonio at the time of the Littlefield commission, he is believed to be the first Texas architect to hold a professional architectural degree. Wahrenberger's design for the Littlefields follows the then-fashionable taste for picturesque eclecticism. The towers and projecting bays make a dramatic impression, as does the material palette: reddish-brown brick, red sandstone trim, granite columns with limestone bases and capitals, polychrome shingles, and cast- and wrought-iron metalwork. Underscoring the image of prosperity is Littlefield's monogram, GWL, on the decorative grilles attached to the front doors.

The plan of the house consists of a central hall flanked by two pairs of rooms on the first floor and bedrooms above. To the rear are the kitchen and servants' quarters, which occupy an addition constructed immediately after the completion of the rest of the house. The principal rooms have high ceilings and tall windows, and those on the ground floor have wide openings between them that maximize flow of air and the circulation of guests. Despite the variety of uses the house has witnessed since it passed to the university following Mrs. Littlefield's death in 1935, many of the original interior finishes remain. Preservation architect and UT School of Architecture faculty member Wayne Bell supervised a restoration of the house in the 1960s.

29. Geography Building
Mark Lemmon, Consulting Architect; Jessen, Jessen, Millhouse and Greeven, Associate Architect, 1952

Originally designed for the journalism program, this building was renovated in 1974 to house other academic units including the Department of Geography. It is one of the earliest buildings designed during Mark Lemmon's tenure as Consulting Architect and occupies a site that Paul Cret had intended for a garden. This appropriation reflects the rapid increase of enrollment following World War II requiring greater campus densities.

Whereas Cret generally reserved symmetrical massing for buildings on an axis or otherwise central to a compositional ensemble, the bold symmetrical massing

Geography Building

Lemmon employed here has no relationship to larger site planning issues. The central volume seems heavy and poorly proportioned in relation to its wings. Stripped classical detailing on the building ranges from fairly conventional motifs (e.g., above the balcony window at the south entry) to Art Deco elements (e.g., above the first floor windows on the flanking wings of the south face). The materials and general style are familiar to the campus, but the sophistication of earlier buildings is greatly diminished.

30. Alice P. Littlefield Dormitory
Herbert M. Greene, 1926

The Littlefield Dormitory is the oldest on-campus residence hall still in use. Throughout its existence, it has housed freshman women in accordance with George Washington Littlefield's bequest, which provided most of the funds for its construction and stipulated that the hall be named for his wife, Alice. Littlefield believed that freshman women would benefit by living in a community focused on smoothing their transition to college life.

Alice P. Littlefield Dormitory

Littlefield had intended that the dormitory be built on lots he owned across the street from his house, but Herbert M. Greene and James M. White located it instead on Dean Keeton Street (formerly 26th Street) in alignment with the private Scottish Rite Dormitory a block to the north. In contrast to his monumental, Neo-Georgian design for the Scottish Rite Dormitory, Greene gave the Littlefield Dormitory a modest, almost rustic character.

The austerity of the Dean Keeton Street facade makes one think twice before trying the front door. The south, campus-facing elevation on the Quad is much more inviting. Greene wrapped the building around three sides of a deep terrace. The effect suggests the garden facade of a villa, but the arrangement also served a pragmatic role, for it provided the majority of rooms an orientation to the prevailing southeasterly breeze. A veranda on the left leads to the social room. The three center bays marking the location of the foyer inside project forward slightly, and the polychrome terra-cotta ornament that frames each opening highlights their importance as the focal point of the composition.

Greene's plan skillfully zoned the more public areas of the dormitory on the first floor of the western half of the building. Their domestic character remains today. The only access to the students' rooms was through a corridor passing the director's apartment to the east of the central foyer. The rooms are small, but Greene sought to offset the cramped dimensions by specifying the use of Murphy beds that could be stowed in the closets. The residents' dining room and its kitchen were located on the lowest level of the east wing (now the site of the Littlefield Patio Cafe).

31. Carothers Hall
Paul Cret, Consulting Architect; Atlee B. and Robert M. Ayres, Architects, 1935

Like Littlefield Dormitory, Carothers Hall is a three-story brick building with a limestone base, a string course at the sill level of the third floor windows, and a tile roof with overhanging eaves, but it and neighboring Andrews Hall, as well as the contemporary Roberts and Prather halls in the men's dormitory group, have a more monumental presence.

The difference is particularly striking when one compares the understated facade of Littlefield Dormitory on Dean Keeton Street with the way Carothers Hall strongly defines Whitis Avenue as a campus boundary. Aligned axially with 25th Street and scaled to appear prominent to those approaching the campus from Guadalupe Street, the entrance is a loggia composed of three arches with limestone surrounds that merge with the ornamental sills and frames of the second-floor windows. On either side of the loggia, carved sills also embellish the ground floor windows, which have elaborate iron grilles. The university seal appears under the eaves at the corners of the building.

Carothers Hall and Diana the Huntress

The hall is named for Asenath Carothers who served as the director of the Woman's Building from its opening in 1903 to 1928. It became a co-ed Honors Residence Hall in 1992.

32. Andrews Residence Hall

Paul Cret, Consulting Architect; Robert Leon White, Architect, 1935

Andrews Residence Hall is easily overlooked by passersby on Whitis or University Avenues. It was the first of the women's dormitories built in accordance with Paul Cret's master plan, but its visibility was compromised in the early 1950s by the construction of what is now the Geography Building on a site Cret had intended as a garden. The stubby ell on the west side of the dormitory marks the location of a wing that was to have bordered the garden along Whitis Avenue.

Containing the lounge above, and, until 1989, the dining room on the basement level, the projecting bay on the east side of the building visually complements the eastern wing of Littlefield Dormitory. Details suggestive of the Spanish Renaissance emphasize key points, such as the

Andrews Residence Hall

entrances and the center of the Whitis Avenue facade. The connections to Carothers and Blanton halls are additions made in the 1950s.

Like the Woman's Building and Littlefield Dormitory, the common spaces of Andrews Hall sought to make the 118 residents feel at home with such domestic touches as wood wainscoting, timber beams, and a fireplace in the lounge. Sundecks on the roofs of the wings were another amenity that found an unanticipated use during the panty raid era of the late 1950s and early 60s. Residents used them as battlements from which they showered undergarments on crowds of men who had marched across campus to beseech their favors.

Andrews became a co-ed building in 1993 when it was incorporated into the Honors Residence Hall Complex. It is named for Jessie Andrews, the first woman to graduate from UT (1886) and the university's first female instructor.

33. Blanton Hall

Mark Lemmon, Consulting Architect; Jessen, Jessen, Millhouse and Greeven, Associate Architect, 1954

The construction of Blanton Hall transformed the Quad from a terrace overlooking University Avenue into an enclosed courtyard. It honors Annie Webb Blanton, whose election as state superintendent of education in 1918 made her the first woman to hold a statewide office in Texas. After two terms in office, she returned to the university where she completed a graduate degree and began her long tenure as a professor of education.

Blanton Hall housed 270 women when it opened, more than twice the number living in Carothers Hall. Its interior finishes were simpler and less evocative of domestic architecture than those of the earlier dormitories, but if Blanton had fewer touches of home, it offered residents a variety of modern amenities including telephones in every room and washing machines and dryers on every floor. In 2000, it became a co-ed Honors Residence Hall.

The exterior expression follows Andrews and Carothers halls in the color of the brick, the limestone framing, and classical ornament at

Blanton Hall

select points, but the details are simpler than those of the earlier buildings, and the eaves have a shallower overhang and are without brackets. A subtle difference in the fenestration is telling. The dormitory rooms of Carothers Hall have large double-hung windows, but Blanton's windows are smaller—an indication that it was designed with central air conditioning, which the older women's residences did not have until the early 1990s.

The Quad, a large, shady greenspace unknown by many who frequent the campus, is overdue for a sensitive reorganization of its walkways, lawns, and lighting. Its centerpiece is the bronze *Diana the Huntress* (1922) by the American sculptor Anna Hyatt Huntington, on a pedestal designed by Paul Cret.

34. Anna Hiss Gymnasium
Herbert M. Greene, LaRoche and Dahl, 1931

Increasingly lost among the large, new buildings encroaching from every direction, Anna Hiss Gymnasium is a relic of a bygone era when men and women resided on different sides of campus and playing fields extended unobstructed from the rear of the gym to Waller Creek. Although it is harder to locate than in the past, the building remains full of life, especially in the evenings when the sounds of jitterbug or salsa fill the air and passersby can glimpse men and women kicking up their heels in the popular dance classes.

Anna Hiss Gymnasium

Anna Hiss, for whom the former Women's Gymnasium was named in 1974, might raise an eyebrow at the dancers' casual intimacy but likely would approve of their commitment to physical fitness. She believed strongly in the importance of athletic activities, informal and competitive, to student life. As the Director of Physical Training for Women from 1921 to 1956, she worked tirelessly to establish a secure place for women's athletics on campus, and the gymnasium stands as testimony to her achievement. It merits preservation as an important artifact of the university's history that continues to provide valuable services to students.

Hiss played a central role in devising the program for the building, which contains gymnasia in parallel wings flanking a grassy courtyard. They are connected on the west side by an entrance wing of almost domestic scale facing the women's dormitory cluster. An indoor swimming pool bounded the east side of the courtyard until 1994, when it was demolished to make room for the Moffett Molecular Biology Building. Beneath the gymnasia are facilities for other sports, including an archery range, locker rooms, offices, and a clubroom with a fireplace.

The gymnasium was an initiative of the Union Project led by the Ex-Students' Association (the Texas Exes) and funded in part by donations. Greene, LaRoche and Dahl created an economical yet elegant design with warm-toned brick walls and broad, red tile roofs complementing Littlefield Dormitory. The three-arched entrance supported by columns with delicate Corinthian capitals invites comparison to the arches on the dormitory's courtyard facade and contrasts with the virile Romanesque arches marking the entrance to Gregory Gymnasium for men.

35. Pharmacy Building

Mark Lemmon, Consulting Architect; Staub and Rather, Architect, 1952; addition: White, Budd, Van Ness Partnership, 1983

The original part of the Pharmacy Building, like the Geography Building, is an early example of the work of Mark Lemmon in his role as Consulting Architect. Unlike the Geography Building, it has much of the sophistication present in the Cret-era buildings, which likely reflects the role of John S. Staub who had worked with Paul Cret on the Texas Memorial Museum. The Pharmacy Building's simple rectangular volume, elegant proportions, and distinct material treatment of base, mid-section, and cap create a classic University of Texas building.

The primary entry from the north fronts a nicely scaled mall that linked the women's dorms to the west with Anna Hiss Gymnasium to the east. Utilizing the slope of the site down to the south, the basement level opened onto grade where there was a parking lot—a new amenity that became important in the 1950s.

Another amenity of the era, air conditioning, also played a prominent role in the building's design. According to a later Pharmacy dean, the faculty of the 1950s

decided to reduce the size of the planned building in order to stay within the budget and still become one of the first structures on campus to be air-conditioned.

An addition to the Pharmacy Building that more than doubled its size was dedicated in 1983 after almost a decade of planning and construction. It demonstrates a case in which choosing not to replicate the architectural vocabulary of adjacent buildings may, in fact, be kinder to the older structures than mimicry. If a second volume similar to the original Pharmacy Building had been jammed into the narrow site to its south, the ensemble would have seemed crowded and very uncomfortable. By lowering the height, avoiding the extra mass of a sloped roof, stepping the building back on the west end and using more subtle materials, the new structure makes the best of a difficult situation.

36. Burdine Hall

Brooks, Barr, Graeber and White, Consulting Architect; Goleman & Rolfe, Associate Architect, 1970

The broad assortment of teaching spaces on the lower two floors and the approximately 125 faculty offices on the top three floors of Burdine Hall were originally planned for the departments of Government, Sociology, and Anthropology. The building was named for John Alton Burdine who had been a vice-president of

Burdine Hall

the university in the controversial years from 1941 to 1945 under President Homer Rainey. He also served as Dean of the College of Arts and Sciences from 1958 until his death in 1967.

Within a short five years after its completion, dissatisfaction with some of Burdine Hall's teaching spaces led to substantial renovations. Several extremely narrow, deep classrooms with steeply sloped floors had become known as "the pits." Student petitions and faculty complaints about the difficulty teachers had communicating with students in the back half of the room provoked the renovation project in which floors were raised and acoustics were improved.

Unfortunately, the renovation did not relieve Burdine Hall from the general scorn that has been heaped on the building throughout its history. The "chicken pox" brick that is pervasive both inside and outside and the disorienting rabbit warren of corridors on the ground floor are but two complaints of many. When the Biomedical

Pharmacy Building

Student Services Building

Engineering Building just to the north was designed, an expansion scheme was planned that presumed the demolition of Burdine Hall in the not too distant future.

37. Student Services Building
Cox/Croslin & Associates, 1997

After passing a referendum in 1991 increasing student fees to help pay for improved facilities for the health center and other student services, the student body felt they had a stake in the nature of the building to be built. By the time the new Student Services Building had been designed and came before the Board of Regents for review, the Student Government had overwhelmingly approved a resolution to delay the project because of objections to its design and site location.

Chief among the students' concerns was the selection of a site across heavily trafficked Dean Keeton Street from the core of the campus where they spent most of their time. The site was also shoehorned around an old apartment building that was being used at the time for the School of Social Work. Building construction was delayed by more than a year because of the controversy, but the design ultimately remained unchanged. However, the dispute did elicit a commitment on the part of then-President Robert Berdahl to launch a campus plan to examine the university's long-term building and land needs in hopes that such site compromises could be avoided in the future.

The design character of the Student Services Building one currently sees from the street gives the same sort of uneasiness about quality that the students observed at the unveiling of its plans. The building seems to naively borrow from some of the worst of campus precedents. Blank, limestone piers recall some of the weaker buildings of the 1950s; their placement is more random and less related to structure than in earlier buildings and their detailing is much thinner. Post-modern stylistic flourishes like the bowed front on the south face feel superficial and dated. The lobby spaces have the character of a shopping mall crossed with a speculative office building.

38. Kinsolving Dormitory

Mark Lemmon, Consulting Architect; Kuehne, Brooks and Barr, Project Architect, 1958

Housing 776 students, Kinsolving Dormitory more than doubled the university's residential accommodations for women. It occupies the site of the house and garden of Episcopal Bishop George Herbert Kinsolving. In the late 1890s, Kinsolving had established a private women's dormitory, Grace Hall (not extant), and chapel, All Saints' Episcopal Church, at the north end of the block. Kinsolving Dormitory completed a chain of private and university residences for women that extended from the Scottish Rite Dormitory on 27th Street to Andrews Residence Hall just north of 24th Street.

The design of Kinsolving Dormitory breaks with the thin rectangular blocks that characterize the university's earlier residential halls. The building is composed

Kinsolving Dormitory

of two, five-story, H-shaped wings linked by a lower central block. This large footprint reflects the university's increasing reliance on mechanical air conditioning and artificial lighting in the 1950s. Although there is no trace of red tile or classical architectural ornament, the window surrounds and the geometrically patterned spandrels and columns marking the entrances on Dean Keeton Street provide a subtle allusion to the detailing of the older dormitories. The aluminum casement windows and exterior stair railings are expressions of the relatively new material's popularity in the decade following World War II.

As a strategy for forging a sense of community among the large resident population, each quadrant of the building functions as a dorm within a dorm served by its own elevator. Each floor has a lounge with late-night study areas, originally equipped with sewing machines and hooded hair dryers. The central block serves all residents with the communal living room, dining facilities, two courtyards, and roof deck for games and sunbathing. With such amenities readily associated with hotels, resorts, and country clubs, the original furnishings projected an image of genteel modernity that posed a striking contrast to the traditional interiors of the older women's residence halls.

Kinsolving was the site of an important episode in the university's coming to terms with desegregation. Although the first African American students were admitted in 1950, campus residence halls were segregated. African American students visiting friends in dorms reserved for whites, such as Kinsolving, were not allowed to use the restrooms or drinking fountains and were to be kept out of sight behind closed doors. In October 1961, students protested the restrictions with a "sit-in" in the lobby of Kinsolving that attracted the attention of news media and inspired additional protests and legal action that eventually forced the Board of Regents to change its policies and desegregate university housing in 1964.

39. Whitis Court
Western units: Mark Lemmon, Consulting Architect; Jessen, Jessen, Milhouse and Greeven, Associate Architects, 1952; eastern units: Fehr and Granger, 1969

Whitis Court occupies the site of the Driskill House, one of the grand late-nineteenth-century homes that once lined Whitis Avenue. For a number of years in the mid-twentieth century, the University Faculty Women's Club occupied the house and contributed to the identity of the northern extension of university as the women's campus. In 1952, the three, two-story brick buildings on the west side of the property were built facing Driskill House, which was demolished approximately fifteen years later to make room for the concrete-frame-and-brick-infill building along Whitis Avenue.

The complex brought together twelve women's cooperative residences, which had occupied a variety of houses scattered on and off campus. Initiated in 1936 by Dean of Women Dorothy Gebauer, the semi-autonomous co-ops offered affordable housing for groups of sixteen to twenty women who shared responsibility for their unit's management and operation. Among them, Almetris House (named for Almetris Duren, see Duren Hall) was notable as a welcoming community for African American women who pioneered the integration of the university in the mid-twentieth century. The co-op era on campus ended in 2003 when the university completed

Whitis Court

appropriation of the buildings for use by the first-year residential interest group program (ResFIGS), which takes advantage of the small size of the units to house incoming students who live and study together. Cooperatives continue to flourish off campus.

The two sets of buildings mark the transition of campus architecture from a simplified historicism to modernist expression. The three units completed in 1952 have red-tile roofs, elements of decorative ironwork, and second-story porches with exposed wooden beams and turned columns. The 1969 building has ornate grilles protecting the ground-level windows but is otherwise a straightforward statement of its structural system.

40. Almetris Duren Hall
Barnes Gromatzky Kosarek Architects, 2005

Located on the site of the home of Emerson Scarbrough, founder of Austin's leading department store in the first half of the twentieth century, Almetris Duren Hall anchors the northwest corner of the campus. Like Kinsolving Dormitory, it represents the state-of-the-art in dormitory design for its time. Its relatively large double-occupancy rooms housing 588 students have private bathrooms and individual thermostats, and the common areas include a variety of lounges, a game room, and exercise facilities. Tightly controlled access points and video cameras replacing the watchful

Almetris Duren Hall

eyes of housemothers address the security concerns of the twenty-first century. The furnishings of the ground-floor lounges foster identity with the romance of rustic (but comfortable) Texas, with hand-hewn study tables of native woods, an abundance of five-pointed stars, and murals of Texas rivers. This iconography recalls the images of rural Texas in the detailing of earlier dorms such as Brackenridge Hall (1932) and contrasts markedly with the mid-century modernism of the original furnishings of the lounges in Kinsolving Dormitory.

Almetris Duren, for whom the dormitory is named, played an important role as a mentor and advocate for African American students attending the university from 1956 to 1980.

41. Jesse H. Jones Communication Center
Ford, Powell and Carson, 1973

The Communication Complex, a three-building group near the northwest corner of the campus housing the College of Communications, was almost a decade old when it was renamed for Houston businessman, publisher, and philanthropist Jesse H. Jones. In its short life before receiving its current appellation, the Jones Center had been called many other names. It was commonly referred to as "old rusty," the "rusty battery" or the "rust box." It was probably the most debated building that had been built on the campus since the Main Building was completed forty years earlier.

The most controversial feature of the complex came as a result of a budget cut required of the architects in the latter stages of design. The lead designer, O'Neil Ford, was one of the most respected architects of his generation in the United States and was an icon in Texas architectural circles. Outspoken and irascible, Ford proclaimed publicly that his clients "wanted it big, big, big. It's bigger than CBS in New York or NBC in Hollywood. Then they wanted it cheap, cheap, cheap, so they cut and cut and cut."

One of the key cuts had a long-lasting impact on Building B, the largest of the three buildings. This nine-story volume addresses Guadalupe Street with a windowless facade necessitated by the broadcast studios and technical facilities

Jesse H. Jones Communication Center

inside. In order to save $150,000, the planned copper skin of the building was replaced with COR-TEN sheathing consisting of steel alloy panels designed to form a thin layer of rust that would seal the face of the metal to prevent subsequent corrosion.

The more aggressive look of the rusty steel compared to the gentle patina of copper was not the only problem created by the replacement. Within a few years, the steel became visibly deteriorated, rusting through in many places. For a decade, the building saw various unsightly remedies and patches until 1990, when a storm blew eleven thirty-pound panels off the building. In 1992, the sheathing was completely replaced with prefabricated, pre-insulated painted steel panels at a cost of three million dollars—twenty times the original cost savings.

Other objections to the complex over the years also stemmed from budget cuts. A shade-giving canopy over the courtyard between the three buildings was omitted at a savings of $45,000, leaving the focus of the complex hot and barren. Ford called it "the single greatest feature of the complex" and mourned its loss.

The four-level William Randolph Hearst Building on the south side of the site was built to accommodate a thirty-two-page offset press and offices for student publications. Classrooms, offices, and other instructional facilities are housed in the seven-level building to the north of the courtyard. The beautifully proportioned concrete work in these two buildings has become sufficiently emblematic of the College of Communication that it will be quoted in the new Belo Center for New Media.

42. Belo Center for New Media
Lawrence Group Architects, 2012 (projected)

Planned to accommodate the extraordinary growth of the College of Communication, this new building across Dean Keeton Street is intended to feel like an extension of the earlier complex. Quotations of the concrete gridded facades with large glass openings from the earlier Ford, Powell and Carson buildings are evident in the south face of the new building. The metal facing on the lower building on Guadalupe Street, built for the KUT radio station, recalls the metal cladding of the original complex as well. The new building makes a more overt gesture to the older parts of the campus, however, than its 1970s predecessor. The traditional brick of the campus as well as the familiar scale and articulation of openings tie it back to the Forty Acres, if only tenuously. The building honors the leaders of the Dallas-based Belo Corp, which owns television stations and cable news channels.

WALK THREE: ENGINEERING AND SCIENCE AREA

Engineering and science buildings fill most of the area adjacent to the northeast quadrant of the Forty Acres. Their seemingly chaotic distribution and appearance are the products of shifts in taste in architecture and planning, increasingly complex building programs, and changes of intention.

The pattern of locating engineering and science on the northern part of the campus was set in the 1920s by Herbert M. Greene and James M. White, who planned the row of buildings for biology, physics, and chemistry along 24th Street and relocated the College of Engineering from its first building (now the Gebauer Building) behind Old Main to Taylor Hall (demolished, 2011) on the east side of Speedway. They oriented Taylor Hall to the south, toward the site of an east mall envisioned as the spine along which future academic buildings could be located as far as Waller Creek. Paul Cret retained the idea in his master development plan of 1933 and designed the Chemical Engineering Building (now Schoch Building) and the Petroleum Engineering Building (now Rapoport Building) as frames for the East Mall at Speedway.

Despite this resolute beginning, the mall's development was piecemeal. The land east of Speedway had been developed privately as a neighborhood of family homes, boarding houses, and shops platted on a grid of streets, none of which aligned with the planned center line of the mall. As the university acquired property in the area, it was put to short-term use and occupied by temporary buildings. The master development plan of 1944 called for clearing the existing streets and buildings, and extending the mall with a row of buildings on each side for the College of Engineering. This scheme was abandoned by the late 1950s, when a building for R.O.T.C. studies (Russell A. Steindam Hall, 1957, designed by Brooks and Barr; demolished 2011) was constructed off the proposed alignment. Construction of the East Mall was finally achieved in the early 1960s. Broader than the South Mall on the Forty Acres, it was planted with a grove of trees criss-crossed by pathways. Modernity, rather than the classicism of the Schoch and Rapoport Buildings, was to be the defining character of the new buildings lining the mall, and Winship Hall (1960) and the Jackson Geological Sciences Building (1967) were built in that spirit.

Thirty years later, however, the analysis of the Pelli Campus Master Plan concluded that these buildings did not frame the open space as effectively as the buildings of the "six pack" lining the South Mall. The Pelli plan set out guidelines for new construction intended to narrow the mall, and these have informed the design of the new Student Activities Center and the Liberal Arts Building, and the redesign of the open space by landscape architects Peter Walker and Associates. In the meantime, the bronze statue of Dr. Martin Luther King, Jr., created by Jeffrey and Anna-Koh Varilla (1999) has provided the mall with a focal element.

One reason the 1944 plan for erecting engineering buildings along the East Mall was abandoned may be that their long, thin footprints, necessary to facilitate natural lighting and cross ventilation, had become obsolete. By the mid-1950s, advances in air conditioning and fluorescent lighting allowed architects to construct thick, blocky structures that could contain the large laboratories engineers and scientists increasingly required for their work. Over the following decades, open land for such buildings was acquired first by taking over the women's sports fields north of 24th Street, then crossing Dean Keeton Street, and, finally, taking over much of the block surrounding Anna Hiss Gymnasium.

The buildings erected on these sites reflect three approaches to context. The first, represented by the Engineering-Science Building (1962) and the J. T. Patterson Laboratories Building (1965) are unabashedly modern in massing and detail but are clad with a brick blend similar to that used for older buildings elsewhere on campus.

The second approach corresponds with the massive building campaign from the late 1960s to the mid 1980s. Robert Lee Moore Hall (1968), Ernest Cockrell, Jr. Hall (1971), Engineering Teaching Center II (1980), and the Chemical and Petroleum Engineering Building (1983) could fit in at any other UT System campus. Their placement and character suggest the architects and university administrators assigned low importance to the relationships among buildings and the spaces between them, much less to their ties to the rest of the campus. Each packages its program of classrooms, labs, and offices into a box wrapped with a grid of piers and spandrels.

The third approach attempts to adopt the materials, compositional features, and details of older campus buildings. The task has proved challenging as architects have had to master unfamiliar styles and apply them to buildings that are larger and fundamentally different in organization from earlier buildings on campus. The Norman Hackerman Building (2010) has a checklist of features that at face value should make it a comfortable fit, but they cannot diminish its bulk, which diminishes neighboring Painter and Welch halls.

The engineering and science area has undergone nearly continuous change over the past thirty years, and more changes will occur in the near future as new instructional and research programs require additional facilities. The challenge for the next generation of architects is to resist formulaic thinking and to seek ways of turning the constraints of tight sites, historic context, and complex programs into opportunities for generating buildings that create a diverse but coherent campus.

Bernard and Audre Rapoport Building

43. E. P. Schoch Building

Paul Cret, Consulting Architect; C. H. Page, Associate Architect; Robert Leon White, Supervising Architect, 1941; renovation: MGM Architects, 1987

44. Bernard and Audre Rapoport Building

Paul Cret, Consulting Architect; C. H. Page, Architect; Robert Leon White, Supervising Architect, 1941; renovation: Graeber, Simmons & Cowan, Inc., 1987

The E. P. Schoch Building and its near twin, the Bernard and Audre Rapoport Building, were built on the eve of the entry of the United States in World War II to house the rapidly expanding programs of the College of Engineering. Paul Cret designed them to frame the planned East Mall, which would not be realized until the early 1960s.

Despite their prominent location, their architecture is a simplified version of the classroom buildings across the street on the Forty Acres, a reflection not only of tight budgets but the beginning of a modernist shift to a more functional aesthetic for engineering buildings. Brick is the dominant material, and the use of limestone has been reduced to horizontal bands along the base, above the first-story windows, and in a frieze under the shallow projecting eaves. With the exception of the projecting entrances, the walls are taut planes with punched openings containing steel-sash windows.

E. P. Schoch Building

Built to house the Department of Chemical Engineering, the E. P. Schoch Building originally contained laboratories for teaching and faculty research and offices. After Chemical Engineering's departure to its new building in 1986, the interior spaces were reorganized to accommodate the departments of Anthropology and Germanic Studies and, later, Geosciences. In 1969 the building was named for Eugene Paul Schoch, the first UT graduate in Chemical Engineering and a faculty member in that department for more than sixty years. Schoch also organized the Longhorn Band and was its director for nineteen years.

Originally called the Petroleum Engineering Building, the Rapoport Building was the first university building in the United States to be dedicated to the subject, which had become a field of vital importance to Texas and to the nation. The labs and other specialized interiors were removed in 1987 when the building was refitted for the Department of Economics. In 1998 it was renamed in honor of noted philanthropists and University of Texas benefactors Bernard and Audre Rapoport.

45. Jackson Geological Sciences Building
Jessen, Jessen, Millhouse and Greeven, Consulting Architect;
Page Southerland Page, Associate Architect, 1967; extension:
O'Connell Robertson & Associates, Inc., 2001

When the Geology Building (renamed in 2005) was constructed in the 1960s, it was seen as a key element in the creation of the East Mall. Its design served that intention well. Like other modern buildings on the campus of the era, it utilized brick and

Cordova Shell limestone but employed them in compositions that were crisp and geometrical. In good modern fashion, ornament on the building was restricted to expression of structure and construction in the form of exposed concrete framing members. The flat roof reduced the bulk of the five-story building volume.

Forty years later, the extension of the structure deliberately undermined those original intentions. The addition stepped forward to narrow and contain the East Mall following the recommendation of the Pelli Campus Master Plan. It re-asserted fidelity to the traditional campus-building idiom

Jackson Geological Sciences Building

of stone base, brick midsection, and red tile roof and even attempted ornament in the form of purely decorative and inaccessible balconies. Though the two pieces of the Jackson Building have little conversation with each other, they each speak eloquently to the values of the respective eras in which they were built.

The building and the Jackson School of Geosciences is named for John A. (a 1940 geology graduate) and Katherine G. Jackson, who bequeathed endowments and assets to the university constituting one of the largest gifts in the history of higher education.

46. Applied Computational Engineering and Sciences Building

Susman Tisdale Gale Architects, 2000

The Applied Computational Engineering and Sciences (A.C.E.S.) building houses faculty and graduate students in computer sciences, electrical engineering, and applied mathematics. It anchors the corner of Speedway and 24th Street and

Applied Computational Engineering and Sciences Building

is the point of reference for the redevelopment of the campus along Speedway to the East Mall. It was funded by the O'Donnell Foundation and realized under a unique arrangement whereby the foundation leased the land from the university, erected the building, and then turned over the keys to the university. The foundation's president, Peter O'Donnell, Jr., played an active role in the building's design and construction.

The architects thoughtfully responded to the design guidelines of the Pelli Campus Master Plan in the massing and articulation of the exterior. The detailing of the facades strikes a balance between the ornamentation of Herbert M. Greene's original wing of Welch Hall and the thin planes and punched openings of the additions to Welch along Speedway.

Although it reinforces the general character of the campus, the building, like many recent structures, is mute as to its function, relying on a small sign set in a plot of grass to indicate its name and purpose. This strategy makes some sense given the importance of flexibility in modern research facilities, but something is lost between the building's stolid exterior and the innovative activities within. Conceived as a setting for interdisciplinary research, the architects designed the building to foster interaction among the researchers. The spacious hallways lined with works of art and numerous lounges are meant to serve as impromptu conference spaces.

47. Bill and Melinda Gates Computer Science Complex and Dell Computer Science Hall
Pelli Clark Pelli Architects, 2012 (projected)

This complex represents the second opportunity the Pelli firm has had to build an individual building in the context of their influential master plan. Two separate wings of academic and research spaces are joined by a glassy, interactive atrium that links Speedway Mall (proposed in their master plan) with a quiet court to the east. Though originally conceived to have large red tile roofs on the two wings, flat roofs were wisely substituted in later stages of design to reduce the bulk of the building so that it would create less scale shift compared to little E. P. Schoch next door. Elements of the ensemble are named for giants of the computer industry, Michael Dell and Bill Gates and Gate's wife, Melinda, whose foundations donated to the building project.

48. Norman Hackerman Building
CO Architects and Taniguchi Architects, 2010

When the old Experimental Science Building was built on the corner of Speedway and 24th Streets in 1952, it was deemed to have "national and international

significance" as a state-of-the-art science research facility. That same year Norman Hackerman, a UT professor since 1945 and one of the first to promote the university as a research center and economic engine for the state, became the chair of the Chemistry Department. He went on to become vice president, provost, and president before he left UT in 1970 to become a longtime president of Rice University.

When the Experimental Science Building was demolished in 2008,

Norman Hackerman Building

Hal C. Weaver Power Plant

it was considered hopelessly outdated. The new building is much larger than its predecessor and is a bit oversized for its site. Its greater width required the loss of most of the north half of a live-oak canopy that once gave 24th Street a gracious, intimate feeling. Its greater height gives it a somewhat looming character compared to the Herbert M. Greene and Paul Cret buildings across the street.

49. Hal C. Weaver Power Plant
Herbert M. Greene, University Architect, 1927

The metaphorical heart of the campus, running day and night with a pulse of sixty cycles per second, the machinery within the Weaver Power Plant complex generates steam and electricity to provide heating and power for everything from dorm-room popcorn poppers to supercomputers and chilling stations for air conditioning. It is named for the professor of mechanical engineering who designed the heating system that served the expansion of the campus in the 1920s.

In keeping with the early-twentieth century practice of treating power plants, water pumping stations, and other components of urban infrastructure as works of civic architecture, Herbert M. Greene designed the plant to stand prominently among the new classroom buildings planned for this portion of the campus. The brick is similar to that of Garrison Hall, for example, and the entrance is framed by a monumental arch embellished by quoins, an ornamental keystone, the university seal, and a pair of ornate iron Strozzi lamps, a popular design inspired by lamps at the

Renaissance Palazzo Strozzi in Florence. High above along the parapet screening the roof are various mechanical symbols and the names of physicists, engineers, and inventors prominent in the development of steam engines and electrical power generation. The tall smokestack is a remnant of the days when the plant was fueled by coal, brought to the site by a railroad spur. Natural gas, delivered by pipeline, fuels the plant today.

Initially, the plant only produced steam. The university purchased electricity from the city of Austin, but the supply in the 1920s was unreliable. In 1937, equipment for large-scale electrical generation went into service, allowing the campus to begin its independence from the city's power grid. As the demand for power has steadily increased over the years, the university's engineers have demonstrated great ingenuity in adding boilers, turbines, chillers, and other heavy equipment in limited space.

A plaque affixed to the stone retaining wall in front of the Power Plant Extension honors Carl J. Eckhardt, a UT alumnus and faculty member in mechanical engineering who merits mention alongside Hal Weaver for his foresight in infrastructure planning. He designed the first phase of the network of utility tunnels, now extending more than six miles, that unobtrusively distribute electricity, steam, water, and other utilities throughout the campus. A far more visible aspect of Eckhardt's inventive legacy is the tradition of lighting the tower of the Main Building to celebrate athletic victories and other notable days on the university calendar.

W. R. Woolrich Laboratories

50. W. R. Woolrich Laboratories

Page Southerland Page, Consulting Architect; Jessen, Jessen, Millhouse and Greeven, Architect, 1958

Willis R. Woolrich was dean of the College of Engineering from 1936 to 1958 and presided over a rapid expansion of its programs, faculty, and undergraduate and graduate enrollment. The building that bears his name extended the engineering campus to the north side of 24th Street and housed new programs in sanitary, aeronautical, electrical, and ceramics engineering on its four principal floors. It is a no-nonsense structure with a reinforced concrete frame infilled by brick spandrels and steel casement windows. The only traces of whimsy are the tiles cladding the walls in the vestibules with colors that proclaim as clearly as the cornerstone plaque that this is a building of the 1950s.

51. Service Building

Mark Lemmon, Consulting Architect; Giesecke, Kuehne and Brooks, Associate Architect, 1952

The Service Building, consisting of wings wrapping around a central delivery yard, was built to house offices and shops of the university's operations and maintenance departments. Its brickwork, red tile roofs, and ornament framing the principal entrances are diminished echoes of the pre-war architecture of Herbert M. Greene and Paul Cret. The building is currently slated for demolition to make way for expansion of the Engineering campus.

52. Engineering-Science Building

Jessen, Jessen, Millhouse, Greeven & Crume, Consulting Architect; Phelps & Dewees & Simmons & Associates, Associate Architect, 1962

The Engineering-Science Building continued the northward expansion of the College of Engineering that had begun with the construction of the Woolrich Laboratories

Service Building

Engineering–Science Building

a few years before. Located on the former site of the women's sports fields, it established an edge for a loose quadrangle of future engineering and science buildings that within a decade extended to Dean Keeton Street.

The massive main building is fully dependent on fluorescent lighting and mechanical climate control. Natural light and ventilation have become amenities rather than necessities and are available only in the offices, classrooms, and small laboratories along the building's perimeter. At its core is a complex arrangement of large laboratories and support areas that often require specific levels of light, temperature, and humidity.

An elegant, if worn, reinforced-concrete pergola connects the main building to a slender tower that formerly housed a pair of particle accelerators. The concrete basin between the two structures was once a water-filled pool that helped shield the apparatus below from solar radiation. The ensemble has a monumental quality that

expresses the glamour of big science in the post-Sputnik era, but its usefulness for
contemporary research has declined, and it now has been marked for demolition in
the near future to make way for expansion to the Engineering campus.

53. J. T. Patterson Laboratories Building
*Brooks, Barr, Graeber and White, Consulting Architect; Jessen, Jessen,
Millhouse, Greeven & Crume, Associate Architect, 1965*

Named for John Thomas Patterson, a distinguished professor of zoology specializing
in the fields of embryology and genetics, this building houses research programs in
the biological sciences. The broad bands of brick, concrete, and glass on its facade
offer little indication of the densely packed plan, which placed offices along the
perimeter and two rows of laboratories
separated by corridors at the center.

J. T. Patterson Laboratories Building

In the spirit of Louis Kahn's
Richards Medical Research Building
at the University of Pennsylvania,
completed in 1965, the primary
staircase is contained within a tower
set apart from the rest of the building.
While the gesture frees space in the
main block for other uses, its greatest
significance is visual. It marks the
entrance, and in the original landscape
plan was the key to a system of
radiating planters that defined a plaza facing the intersection of Speedway and 24th
Street. For persons willing to take the stairs rather than ride the elevators, the tower's
straightforward, richly textured materials (brick and concrete) and broad views of
the campus from each landing provide relief from the drab corridors and utilitarian
laboratories.

54. Robert Lee Moore Hall
*Brooks, Barr, Graeber and White, Consulting Architect; George L. Dahl,
Associate Architect, 1968*

As the massive Beauford H. Jester Center neared completion at the southern end
of Speedway in 1968, construction of another high-rise structure began three blocks
to the north. Named for Robert Lee Moore, a professor of mathematics, the L-shaped
building has a fourteen-story north wing and a ten-story east wing set above

Robert Lee Moore Hall

several subterranean levels. It contains classrooms, the John M. Kuehne Physics Mathematics Astronomy Library, and laboratories and offices for those departments.

The building stands awkwardly presenting an abrupt change of scale, character, and color in comparison to its original neighbors, the Engineering-Science and Patterson Laboratories buildings to the east and south and Anna Hiss Gymnasium across Speedway to the west (now hidden behind the Moffett Molecular Biology Building). Its architectural vocabulary of tan bricks and gridded facades containing wide, deeply recessed windows derives from the Music Building East (1969), by the same designers. The most notable feature is the composition of angled piers and multilevel openings along the plaza side of the north wing. The gesture is not unique to the UT campus. Similar compositions appear on many public buildings of similar vintage around the country. All speak to the powerful impression the new Boston City Hall (Kallman, McKinnell and Knowles, 1963–1968) had on American architects in the late 1960s and early 1970s.

The library and most heavily used classrooms are located on the first four floors, which are connected by escalators. Like commercial office buildings planned to maximize rentable area, public space is minimal. The ground-floor snack bar and seating on the crowded escalator landings are improvised and inadequate for the building's large population of students, staff, and faculty. More recent buildings on campus, such as A.C.E.S., are more generous in the provision of areas conducive to the informal learning and social interactions that occur outside classrooms and offices.

55. Ernest Cockrell Jr. Hall

Brooks, Barr, Graeber and White, Consulting Architect;
Page Southerland Page, Associate Architect, 1971

Ernest Cockrell, Jr. was an engineering alumnus who went on to a distinguished career as an oilman, investor, Houston civic leader, and philanthropist. In addition to this building, the Cockrell School of Engineering is named in his honor. Cockrell Hall houses classrooms, offices, and the McKinney Engineering Library.

The building offers no acknowledgment of its academic purpose or location on the UT campus. Its bland bulk could be placed unnoticed among the state office buildings in the state capitol complex south of campus. Questions of context aside, the building's layered composition of tan brick piers, spandrels, and recessed windows, creates a play of light and shadow across the facades and projects a strong visual order that reads clearly from a distance.

Like so many buildings of its time, however, there is no mediation between large-scale order and human scale. The main entrance is simply inserted into the overall pattern of solids and voids and depends on the stairs approaching it and the lettering above to signal its presence. A greater misfortune is the barren street facade below the engineering plaza along Dean Keeton Street that traps pedestrians between a sheer retaining wall and heavy traffic.

The bridge spanning Dean Keeton Street, built in 1975, carries utilities as well as pedestrians. Like the other walkways and plazas in this part of campus, it solves a

Ernest Cockrell Jr. Hall

particular problem, crossing a busy street in this case, but contributes little to a larger vision of pedestrian circulation and public space.

56. Engineering Teaching Center II
Page Southerland Page, 1980

Engineering Teaching Center II houses the Department of Mechanical Engineering and the Texas Materials Institute. Its massing, brickwork, and recessed fenestration closely resemble Cockrell Hall, which was completed a decade earlier, but the overall effect

Chemical and Petroleum Engineering Building (left) and Engineering Teaching Center II (right)

of the facades is much flatter due to the positioning of the piers in the same plane as the spandrels instead of being set forward. Renovation of the ground floor in 2008 opened up the lobby and transformed a cramped study area into a student lounge with a wall of windows looking out over Waller Creek. Its name, the T-Room, refers to the first dean of Engineering, T. U. Taylor, and the legendary lounge hand-dug by students beneath old Taylor Hall in the 1950s.

57. Chemical and Petroleum Engineering Building
Calhoun, Tungate, Jackson, and Dill, 1983

Dedicated in 1988, this building was built to house departments that had outgrown Schoch and Rapoport halls. Its architecture employs the brickwork and recessed fenestration of Engineering Teaching Center II and Cockrell Hall, but unlike them, it addresses its surroundings with a broad portico that provides a transition to a shallow plaza and a bermed lawn. The effectiveness of this gesture as public space, however, is compromised by a pair of stairwells that prevent direct access from the portico to the plaza.

Petroleum Engineering occupies the western half of the building. Among its laboratories and offices are two of the most unusual spaces on campus. An area of the basement contains a network of narrow, low-ceilinged passages simulating the rooms and support pillars of a coal mine. Unused today, the space was intended as a teaching tool for classes in coal mining technology. Elsewhere in the building is a shaft extending from the basement to the roof that can be outfitted with pipes and

Animal Resources Center

pumps to simulate the operation of oil and gas wells. At the bottom is the head of a two-hundred-foot dry well that allows students to work at full scale with valves and other equipment.

58. Animal Resources Center
Hoff Blackstone Strode Architects, 1975; extension: White, Budd, Van Ness Partnership, 1994

A row of trees and the steeply sloping site screen the building from Speedway. Only a discrete sign indicates its purpose: housing thousands of vertebrate animals utilized in the university's teaching and research programs. In addition to the facilities for animals, the building contains laboratories, offices, and meeting rooms.

Its massing is prismatic with broad expanses of dark brick walls punctured by recessed windows recalling the nearby engineering buildings. In a nod to the older buildings on campus, the sharp lines are broken at the top of the central block by an unadorned frieze, projecting cornice, and hipped roof.

59. North Office Building
Overland Partners, 2002

This L-shaped building wraps gracefully around a pre-existing live oak tree and represents a sensitive response to the planning directions and the design guidelines

North Office Building

outlined in the Pelli Campus Master Plan. A gently scaled arcade faces the tree on two sides, providing the kind of opportunity for casual interaction that is evident in the best of the buildings on the Forty Acres.

The stone base, brick mid-section and crowning red-tile roof follow a familiar vocabulary, but, in detail, the building has some interesting invention. Horizontal steel bands articulate the seam between the stone and brick, indicating that this is not a load-bearing masonry wall. Cantilevered brackets supporting the deep eaves are rendered frankly as steel. They seem authentic and not simply a stylistic flourish.

60. Sarah M. and Charles E. Seay Building
Cesar Pelli Associates and Page Southerland Page, 2001

The first new building to be constructed as part of the Pelli Campus Master Plan, the Seay Building allowed the plan's authors to flesh out their work in terms of architectural intentions. It also provided an anchor for the new north campus development on the prominent corner of Speedway and Dean Keeton streets that was a critical element of the master plan.

Built primarily to house the Department of Psychology, the U-shaped structure was also planned to accommodate the Child Development and Family Relations program with its Lab School (a nursery for three- and four-year-olds). The central portion of the U along Dean Keeton Street contains primarily faculty and administrative offices. The wing to the west contains mostly classrooms and the wing to the east primarily houses labs so that each floor conveniently integrates office, teaching, and research spaces.

The beautifully landscaped courtyard at the heart of the composition is surrounded by terraces that provide pleasant spaces for lunch or casual interaction. Gracious staircases at the intersections of the building's wings provide views to the courtyard as well as encouragement to take the stairs rather than elevators.

Austin Gleeson, chair of the Master Planning Committee and longtime chair of the Faculty Building Advisory Committee said of the building as it began construction, "It's probably about the best compromise you can have between modern building

Sarah M. and Charles E. Seay Building

techniques and the style of the original Forty Acres." Indeed, many of the familiar motifs of the Gilbert, Greene, and Cret eras are present. A brick mid-section and a red tile roof top a cream-colored limestone base. Regular rhythms of punched windows articulate all of the facades. Colorful soffits accent the underside of the deep roof overhangs.

Though there are nods to tradition, in each case the motif is tweaked slightly to make it fresh and more contemporary. The brick is banded and textured in a new way. Dominantly horizontal mullions in the windows set them apart from their predecessors. Soffits are flat and abstract rather than heavy and structural as in earlier buildings. The composite effect is to make a building that is certainly deferential to the fabric of the old campus but also has a character of its own.

The building is named for two longtime donors to the university who contributed funds specifically for the building's construction. The Seays first met as UT students in the 1930s and attributed much of their financial success in insurance and insurance brokerage to their university experience.

61. Neural Molecular Science Building
Overland Partners and Watkins Hamilton Ross Architects, Inc., 2002

The Neural Molecular Science Building commands a dominating presence on Dean Keeton Street by its location near a topographical high point, the placement of its six-story mass very near the street edge, its large floor-to-floor dimensions (required by contemporary lab spaces), and its strong symmetry. That symmetry, curiously, neither acknowledges any axis in the larger campus environment nor signals a primary entry.

The main entry to this huge building is, in fact, modestly located on its west wing. Once inside, there is no real lobby and the elevators are distant. Most of the interior is, in fact, endless beige corridors with doors that open automatically, elevators

Neural Molecular Science Building

that talk to their riders, and lots of makeshift notes taped to the walls giving room numbers for important destinations. Away from the public eye, however, the labs are often light-filled spaces with dramatic views.

62. Biomedical Engineering Building
3D/International, Inc., 2008; south wing expansion: Parsons, 2010

The Student Health Center that had occupied this prominent corner site since 1950 was demolished in 2005. The replacement project, like several of its contemporaries, sought to replicate the character of the Cret-era buildings, but at a significantly larger scale and on a tight site.

The general massing of the building vaguely resembles the Texas Union and Goldsmith Hall, with a tower element at the northwest corner and lower wings to the east and south. Though clearly designed in deference to its predecessors, the building does not begin to match the richness of detail seen in earlier campus buildings.

Masonry walls that in prior buildings might have had a depth of fourteen or sixteen inches from glass to outer edge of the stone are flattened to four to six inches here. The richly articulated soffit embellishments of the campus' historic buildings are reduced to flat plaster painted with multicolored stripes. Token porches, whose

Biomedical Engineering Building

five-foot depth is neither gracious nor usable for any occupation, may only be compared superficially to the entry portals of Sutton Hall or even Calhoun Hall of the late 1960s.

63. Louise and James Robert Moffett Molecular Biology Building
Harper, Kemp, Clutts and Parker, 1997

Before its doors opened, the Molecular Biology Building provoked two raging controversies that pitted regental and administrative perspectives against the sentiments of faculty and students. In many ways, it was the difficulties that arose in the planning of this building, along with the Student Services Building of the same era, that provoked the university to create the Pelli Campus Master Plan.

The first controversy stemmed from the plan to demolish the east wing of historic Anna Hiss Gymnasium, which housed a swimming pool, in order to assemble a site of the preferred width for the new laboratory building. Vocal faculty and community preservation leaders protested this loss. Advocates for barrier-free design decried the closing of the only accessible pool on the campus at the time. Those campaigning for the new building emphasized the dimensional requirements of modern laboratories and the importance of the site's proximity to related science

Louise and James Robert Moffett Molecular Biology Building

buildings. They considered the preservation of the other three wings of the gym to be a judicious compromise.

The second controversy arose from the proposal to name the building for James Robert (Jim Bob) Moffett and his wife, Louise. Moffett was a 1961 UT graduate and football player who was CEO of Freeport-McMoRan, a company that had come under fire for allegedly irresponsible environmental practices both in the United States and abroad.

The final budget and design of the building also became problematic just as construction was to begin. Originally designed with a skin of "jumbo brick," the exterior materials were upgraded to a combination of Cordova Shell limestone and Lueders limestone when the building's threat to established campus architecture became an issue. The increased price caused by the delay and more expensive materials required last-minute acquisition of additional funds.

The resulting building is a big laboratory box with an expensive skin and a few contextual flourishes. Its grand symmetry, which makes little sense on the Speedway facade, is a reflection of the central axis of the remnants of little Anna Hiss behind it. A sally port capped by a big swooping curve celebrates the axis at a scale much grander than its gentle forbearer. On the building's west side there is a large porch addressing the Anna Hiss courtyard. It is faced, quite anachronistically, in brick that is meant to look like a nod to the gym, but, in fact, just alienates the porch from the rest of the building.

64. Larry R. Faulkner Nano Science and Technology Building

Jennings-Hackler & Partners, 2005

This oddly proportioned building was squeezed between the remnants of historic Anna Hiss Gymnasium to the north, the Moffett Molecular Biology Building to the east, the Pharmacy Building to the north, and the old Experimental Science Building (which was slated for demolition at the time) to the south. It is now grafted onto the Hackerman Building, its new southern neighbor.

The only frontage for the building was originally a lane used primarily for loading. It is not illogical then that the apparent "face" of the building on the north side is symmetrically composed with a prominent loading dock as its focus.

Larry R. Faulkner Nano Science and Technology Building

WALK FOUR: LARGE CAMPUS-WIDE MAGNETS

Just off the southeast corner of the Forty Acres three large magnets of campus life converge at the corner of Speedway and 21st Street: Gregory Gymnasium, Perry-Castañeda Library, and Beauford H. Jester Center. Each building is large and imposing, handles thousands of student trips in and out of their doors every day, and represents a major facet of college life at The University of Texas at Austin.

Gregory Gymnasium was the first major building (not counting the stadium) outside the Forty Acres. Almost "off-campus" at the time of its construction, it was a bridge between town and gown serving as entertainment venue and spectator sports center as well as a place for student recreational activities. Since it was the men's gym, it offered a logical adjacency for a series of men's dormitories, thereby containing the campus' sweat and testosterone in a single, manageable place.

As the university grew rapidly in the 1960s, and it became necessary to significantly increase student housing, the men's playing fields became an obvious location for new dormitories. Since housing was now co-ed, there was no reason to divide men's and women's housing on opposite sides of the campus, and the gargantuan Jester Center was born.

Almost a decade later, parking lots across 21st Street from the School of Business became the site for a new main library. Perry-Castañeda Library matched the other magnets in scale and swagger creating a sort of architectural battlefield among the behemoths.

Though each of the three magnet buildings is inwardly focused and stylistically self-centered, there is synergy among them. During class hours, thousands of students dart back and forth among home, classroom, recreation, and study facilities. From dinnertime to late at night, they migrate more casually between dining halls, library duty, and intramural sports.

These magnets have attracted other campus-wide functions to the area. In terms of location, the Blanton Museum is well situated, but its architecture does not respond fully to the intense pedestrian activity nearby. The building appears as a disengaged and isolated architectural event that does little to entice drop-in traffic. By contrast, the new Student Activities Center promises to be more engaging. Nestled among old live oaks just north of Gregory Gym, its orientation taps into the pedestrian flow enticing students to relax in its inviting cafes, courtyards, and lounges. These informal community spaces as well as the ones proposed for Speedway Mall by Peter Walker Partners promise to take full advantage of the potential energy collected by the three magnets.

Gregory Gymnasium

65. Gregory Gymnasium

Herbert M. Greene, LaRoche and Dahl, 1930; extension: Jessen, Jessen, Millhouse and Greeven, Consulting Architect, Morris, Crain and Anderson, Associate Architect, 1963; renovation: F & S Partners, 1996

As the university acquired land to the east and southeast of the Forty Acres, it built "shacks," cheap unpainted pine structures, on the new acreage to accommodate its growing needs. The largest of these was a men's gymnasium (1916) on Speedway that was both infamous for its poor construction quality and dear to the university community for the fact that it provided a place for large lectures, performances, and athletic events. When Will Rogers lectured on the campus, he told his audience he did not object to speaking in the gym because he had spent most of his life in barns and was accustomed to them. It was something of a relief to university officials when this firetrap burned to the ground early in the morning of Sunday, March 25, 1928, with no injuries or loss of life.

The event greatly assisted the fund-raising effort led by General T. W. Gregory to build a permanent auditorium-gymnasium as part of a four-building Union Group sponsored by the Ex-Students Association (Texas Exes). Gregory, for whom the building would be named, received his law degree from UT in 1885 and became U.S. Attorney General under President Woodrow Wilson. Deeply loyal to the university, he served as regent from 1899 to 1907 and was president of the Texas Exes from 1926 to 1927.

The new auditorium-gymnasium seated 7,500 people for concerts, lectures, and dramatic performances with a large stage and backstage facilities. The facility also provided ample space for intercollegiate basketball games, recreational sports, and physical education classes. It included an indoor swimming pool, handball courts, training rooms, and lecture halls, as well as showers and lockers for four thousand men.

By its size, location, and configuration, the gym soon became the heart of student life. It was the scene for the legendary lines and bureaucratic frustrations of registration in the heat of the late summer. It was home to "Round-up" revues, pep rallies, and graduation. High school students from across the state converged on the gym each spring for state basketball championship tournaments. Both in its functional arrangement of spaces and in its memorable architectural character, the building did an excellent job of creating a crucible for important events and memories.

Architecturally, Herbert M. Greene's design for Gregory Gymnasium departed from the vocabulary Cass Gilbert had established for academic buildings twenty years earlier. Greene realized that the palazzo format was inappropriate for this very different building type with its much larger spaces, longer structural spans, and more raucous activities. He rejected hipped roofs in favor of bold repeating gables and replaced deep overhangs with clipped eaves. Exposed board-formed concrete created a simple, massive base and huge, modern, steel-sash windows provided generous light and ventilation. The primary ornament was not in terra-cotta or carved stone but in patterned brickwork and geometric zigzags in concrete spandrels. The building was vaguely Romanesque Lombard in character with its diagonal row of relieving arches and corbel tables, but it was true to no style as a whole. It was a big, tough, flexible workhorse of a building fit for a growing university.

Inside, Gregory Gymnasium had the same simple, muscular character demonstrated on the outside. The walls of the lobby and the big gym/auditorium were made of local Austin common brick—a softer, lighter, more irregular masonry than on the exterior. Steel trusses were exposed in the big, central space, and the construction of the dark wood trophy cases in the lobby was straightforward with just a bit of simple painted ornament.

In 1963, the addition of an annex on its south side almost doubled Gregory Gymnasium in size. The new structure followed the original organizational format with a vast, long-span space for basketball and volleyball on the upper floor and handball and racquetball courts, training rooms, and lockers below. This vertical distinction was signaled on the exterior of the building by a series of concrete T's with an elaborately patterned brick in-fill on the ground floor capped by solid panels of plain brick above.

In 1996, the entire building was renovated. Though no substantial new area was added, an extensive reorganization of uses and spaces (especially on the

Gregory Gymnasium interior

lower floors) converted a labyrinthine maze of corridors and passages into a clear, open functional diagram. The main entrance to the complex was located at the joint between the original building and the 1963 annex. A three-story, sky-lit concourse was inserted to create clearer circulation routes and to provide a social core. The south face of the original building (which had been covered by the 1963 addition) was exposed and restored.

Ice-cold air and a health club/spa ambiance replaced the sound of giant pre–air-conditioning fans and the "comfortable tennis shoes" feeling of the old Gregory. The original 1930 gym/auditorium building remained significantly intact, but the 1963 annex was radically altered by the replacement of most of the patterned brick panels on the lower floor with glass, the insertion of a day-lit running track above, and the addition of massive new fire stairs.

Through three distinctly different cycles of its architectural life, Gregory Gymnasium has retained its status as one of the most important buildings on the campus for student life. It is currently a hub of informal social interaction as well as a vital base for fitness, sports, and recreation. Whether getting a tan under the palm trees of the new outdoor pool, sweating through an intense intramural basketball contest, rooting for the women's volleyball team, working out in the state-of-the-art weight room, or watching an away football game on television in one of the lounges, thousands of students, faculty, and staff make Gregory Gymnasium an integral part of their life at UT every day.

66. Perry-Castañeda Library
Bartlett Cocke & Associates, Inc. and Phelps & Simmons & Associates, 1977

The third main library building constructed on the UT campus (after Battle Hall in 1911 and the Main Building's library which opened in 1934), the Perry-Castañeda Library (known familiarly as PCL) was thought to be the third largest library building in the United States at the time of its opening. It boasted more than half a million square feet, contained more than seventy miles of bookshelves and had a capacity of 3.25 million volumes.

Two substantial changes in modern library usage helped shape the new building and differentiated it from its predecessors. First, the PCL was designed as a substantially open-stack library with direct user access to most books—a big change from the previous facilities where books had to be requested by users and retrieved by library staff. In this way, it resembled the innovative Undergraduate Library (located in what is now the Flawn Academic Center) that had been operating as an open-stack library for almost fifteen years.

Second, whereas the two prior main libraries had emphasized vertical storage of books in stacks, the PCL emphasized the more contemporary practice of creating

Perry-Castañeda Library

large horizontal spaces, which reduced subject and physical segregation of books and facilitated the movement of readers, staff, and books from section to section. The arrangement also allowed for more integration of reading study spaces with book storage areas.

Although the architects and library administrators credited the rather odd shape of the building in plan to functional response and an effort to reduce the apparent mass of the huge structure, users immediately made a connection between the building's footprint and the shape of the State of Texas. Many people also erroneously view the dominant exterior material as concrete, which would have been a departure from the limestone and brick commonly used on the campus. In fact, the exterior is indeed limestone, but it is a much grayer, highly textured Indiana limestone applied in panels rather than the smooth, cream-colored, coursed Texas limestone used on most UT buildings.

One of the most impressive aspects of the PCL for its time is its climate-responsive design. Though there is a large amount of glass, deep vertical fins block the low east and west sun from entering the building and horizontal sunshades on the south face protect it from midday sun during the hotter portions of the year. Using a vocabulary similar to Le Corbusier's famous Secretariat Building (1953) in Chandigarh, India, the architects create a striking play of light and shadow while also offering a practical defense against the hot Texas sun.

Though there is much to admire in the functional innovations, the ambitious use of materials, and the climate responsiveness of the PCL, it has never been a popular building on the campus. Its daunting scale (especially on the very exposed east side), its fortress-like feel, and its harsh and often confusing interiors have never inspired the kind of affection generated by Battle Hall or the library in the Main Building. A modest interior renovation on the ground floor in 2007 made an attempt to soften the building, but it still retains its image as a big, tough, anonymous place to work or study.

67. University Teaching Center
Graeber, Simmons & Cowan, Inc., 1984

Although its exterior skin makes it look like a part of Perry-Castañeda Library, the University Teaching Center was built as an extension of the School of Business across 21st Street providing badly needed instructional space, which also serves other units of the university. The pedestrian bridge was part of the project, even though the architectural character implies little connection.

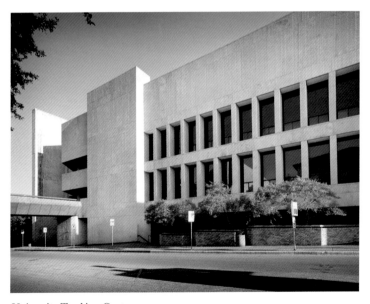

University Teaching Center

Its twenty-six theater-style classrooms have mostly identical pie-shaped plans. Vertical circulation is primarily outdoors via stairs and escalators located off an internal courtyard. Although the facility can accommodate 3,500 students at any given time, it is shockingly devoid of spaces for them to mingle or chat. Its spatial orientation seems to lend itself to herding large numbers of students in and out of class rather than offering an interactive academic environment.

68. George I. Sanchez Building

Wilson, Morris, Crain and Anderson, 1975

Longer than a football field, this five-level structure was built to bring together units of the College of Education that previously had been housed in seven buildings across the campus. It was planned to accommodate four thousand undergraduate and graduate students and was one of the last of the series of buildings constructed in response to the enrollment boom of the 1960s.

The Dean of Education at the time proudly called the building an "attractive warehouse." It was intended to provide flexible space wherein partitions could be freely moved as needs changed. The only fixed elements were stairwells, elevators, escalators, and rest rooms.

George I. Sanchez Building

Such open classrooms were all the rage in public schools in the 1970s. They were intended to facilitate flexible groupings of students, versatility in teaching style, and the creation of diverse learning environments. But here, as in many schools across the country, the arrangement, attractive in theory, became controversial in practice with faculty and students objecting to noise, distractions, and the inability to control lighting. One of the most innovative teaching spaces was the Al Kiva on the lowest level featuring four staggered levels of moveable chairs and tables arranged in a sort of "theater-in-the-round." There was no blackboard, and the center of the room was the focus of attention.

The bright and colorful interior was strikingly different from other campus buildings. Many partitions between corridors and workspaces were floor-to-ceiling clear glass with siding doors. Departments and levels were color-keyed in a rainbow of hues and brightly colored chairs contrasted sharply with white tables and desks and dark grey carpet.

Consistent with the values of its college, this was one of the first buildings on the campus to utilize barrier-free design. Vertical circulation, water fountains, and restrooms were designed to accommodate wheelchairs, and room numbers and other signs were recessed to be friendlier for blind users.

Today, the flexibility built into the building has been used primarily to undo many of the innovations of the 1970s. The open classrooms have been enclosed by doors and partitions. Even the Al Kiva has rows of seats in its sunken center and a fairly conventional "front" has been established with a lectern at one end. Most of the colorful walls have been replaced by expanses of beige, and many of the glass partitions have been frosted to give added privacy in workspaces.

Though not as distinctive as it was in its earlier life, the Sanchez Building retains a striking openness and sense of accessibility. The wide, glass-lined halls, as well as the generous lounges and vertical circulation spaces, give a feeling of communication and collegiality. The building's namesake, George I. Sanchez, taught in the College of Education from 1940 to 1972 and was a pioneer in the promotion of bilingual public education.

69. AT&T Executive Education and Conference Center
HKS, Inc. and Lake | Flato Architects, Inc., 2008

The two-block University Avenue has long played a role as a front door to UT because of its axial relationship to the Littlefield Fountain, the South Mall, and the Main Building. Until 2008, it had been a motley collection of functions and buildings lining a poorly maintained streetscape, but the construction of the AT&T Center provoked improvements that have made it a fitting approach to the monumental southern gateway to the campus.

AT&T Executive Education and Conference Center

The AT&T Center is a combination of a 300-room hotel, restaurant, and bar facing University Avenue and a conference center facing Whitis Avenue to the west. At the center of the composition is a beautifully scaled courtyard that is the most significant architectural gesture of the complex.

70. Jack S. Blanton Museum of Art
Kallman, McKinnell and Wood Architects with Booziotis & Company Architects, 2003

For decades, the University Art Museum, later known as the Archer M. Huntington Art Gallery after its first benefactor, occupied cramped quarters in the Art Building and the Harry Ransom Center. In the mid-1990s, generous financial donations for consolidating the collections in a new museum came from Mari Michener (who with her husband, the author James Michener, had donated many works of art to the museum) and from the Houston Endowment, Inc. The building was named in honor of Jack S. Blanton, who received both undergraduate and law degrees from UT and served as regent (1985–91) and chair of the Board of Regents (1987–89).

The design of the building provoked controversy and reflection regarding the degree to which new construction on campus should adhere to the forms

established by Cass Gilbert, Herbert M. Greene, and Paul Cret. After an exhaustive screening process that identified three distinguished finalists, including Steven Holl and Antoine Predock (architect of Austin's City Hall, 2004), the university awarded the commission to the Swiss firm Herzog & de Meuron Architekten, which was receiving international acclaim for transforming an abandoned power station in London into the Tate Modern. In 1999, the architects' preliminary schemes drew the ire of some regents for straying from their interpretation of the architecture design guidelines incorporated in the recently adopted Pelli Campus Master Plan. The disagreement turned ugly, and the architects resigned the commission despite President Larry Faulkner's efforts to mediate a resolution. Widespread coverage of the incident in the press portrayed the university in an unflattering light, and the architects' receipt of the prestigious Pritzker Prize several months later underscored the sense that a great opportunity had been lost. Nevertheless, the museum's director, Jesse Hite, and its benefactors regrouped and conducted a second selection process, choosing the prominent Boston firm, Kallman, McKinnell and Wood, which managed to appease the disgruntled regents.

Located on Martin Luther King Boulevard across from the Bob Bullock Texas State History Museum at what had once been the intersection with Speedway, the Blanton marks a gateway to the campus. Herzog & de Meuron had keyed a preliminary scheme to the movement of people entering campus through a low, highly transparent building with an undulating roof. Kallman, McKinnell and Wood split the museum into two parts separated by a trapezoidal plaza designed by Peter Walker & Partners. The narrow plaza, filled with a grove of cedar elms, allows views into campus and out toward the Capitol, but it is more of a passageway than a gathering point.

The smaller of the two buildings, completed in 2008, is named for Houston businessman and alumnus Edgar A. Smith. It contains the museum shop, cafe, and lecture hall on the ground floor and classrooms and offices above. The Mari and James A. Michener Gallery Building, opposite, opened in 2006. Both are clad with slabs of smooth Cordova Cream limestone articulated by large panels of Cordova Shell limestone. Arcaded porticos face the plaza, and regulation red tile roofs terminate the broad eaves. The palette recalls buildings of the Cret era, but the handling of materials—the scale and finish of the masonry panels, the detailing of the corbelled cornice and the eaves—is unmistakably of the twenty-first century.

At the heart of the Michener Gallery Building, a skylight-covered atrium echoes the building's trapezoidal plan. An arcade along two sides providing access to the galleries for temporary exhibitions reprises the exterior portico, and a grand staircase facing the longest side leads to the galleries of the permanent collection on the second floor. By itself, the stark white space is like an empty stage. It has been brought to life by Teresita Fernández's installation, *Stacked Waters* (2009), which covers the lower walls with blue acrylic tiles that suffuse the room with an aquatic glow.

Jack S. Blanton Museum of Art

Beauford H. Jester Center

71. Beauford H. Jester Center
*Brooks, Barr, Graeber and White, Consulting Architect; Jessen, Jessen,
Millhouse, Greeven & Crume with John Linn Scott, Associate Architects,
1969*

A persistent urban legend claims the architects for the massive Beauford H. Jester
Center specialized in prisons. This is not the case. The firms responsible for its
design are the authors of numerous buildings on the UT campus. Nevertheless,

the expanses of blank wall and tiers of small windows surrounded by heavy limestone frames do suggest a facility that sequesters its residents from the outside world.

Such an intention was far from the minds of those who conceived the dormitory. At the dedication in September 1969, Regent Frank N. Ikard spoke of how it was to "provide numerous opportunities to interrelate living experience and the learning experience." The Jester Center was a bold experiment intended to foster a sense of community among the university's newest students.

By the mid-1960s, enrollment had risen to 32,000, but the provision of on-campus housing had lagged. Besides exacerbating the persistent housing shortage, the burgeoning population elicited concerns that students, particularly freshmen, were getting lost in the crowd. In 1965, the Board of Regents formed a committee, which for the first time included student representation, to prepare recommendations for a new dormitory inspired by the house model. Familiar in private universities, this type of dormitory combined residential and academic facilities, and to this end Jester was designed to include a large lecture hall, classrooms, language labs, a library reading room, and offices for faculty and student services in addition to residential floors. Apartments for faculty had been included in the preliminary plans but were eliminated due to budgetary limitations. However, unlike the typical college house with one or two hundred residents, the Jester Center was built on an unprecedented scale, housing approximately 3,000 students. At the time of completion, it was the largest college dormitory in North America.

The planning of the Jester Center coincided with nationwide interest in the use of high-rise buildings on college campuses to meet the demands of rapidly growing enrollments. These structures often were designed as freestanding towers in park-like settings, such as Harvard's Peabody Terrace (Sert, Jackson & Gourley, 1962–1964) and the Southwest Quadrangle at the University of Massachusetts (Hugh Stubbins & Associates, ca. 1966). Jester's proximity to the men's dormitory group led its architects to follow a different strategy. They placed two towers of ten and fourteen stories amid courtyards surrounded by three- and five-story buildings with Cordova Shell limestone trim and red tile roofs responding to the scale and materials of the older dormitories along 21st Street. The arrangement reduces the towers' presence on the street, but nothing tempers their sheer rise within the courtyards.

The main entrances to the public areas of Jester are between the perimeter buildings on the northwest corner of the site. They lead into an L-shaped interior street that parallels Speedway and 21st streets. Three stories tall under a slanting roof with day lighting from high clerestory windows, the street has first-floor shops (not as many as originally planned), restaurants, post office, and a large lecture hall that doubles as a movie theater. (The piece of pressed tin affixed above the box office is a fragment of B. Hall, the first dormitory on campus.) Galleries indicate the continuation of the public spaces on the second and third levels and lead to the classrooms, student services offices, and the main dining halls. Brick, concrete, and red floor tiles constitute the primary materials. They are durable but relentlessly hard, visually and acoustically, and do not easily accommodate furnishings that invite one to linger.

The Jester experiment has had mixed results. Despite ongoing efforts to facilitate interchange between students and faculty, the scale of the enterprise does not permit the same degree of interaction that smaller residential colleges offer. It can also overwhelm students accustomed to the low population densities of small towns or suburbs. Other students, however, find the environment invigorating, sometimes to excess, as *Esquire* magazine reported in an article describing rowdy life in the dorm in February 1979.

Governor Beauford H. Jester, for whom the Center is named, was an alumnus of the university who served as a member and chairman of the Board of Regents during the crucial years surrounding the conception and initial implementation of Paul Cret's master plan. Elected governor of Texas in 1946, he died in office three years later.

Men's Dormitory Group

The first effort to provide student housing on campus came in 1890 when San Antonio banker and UT regent George Washington Brackenridge funded construction of a dormitory for fifty-eight male students just east of Old Main. Expanded to accommodate one hundred students in 1900, the fabled B. Hall served as a dormitory until the mid-1920s, when it was converted into an academic building. Its residents were moved into renovated space in the Little Campus (now the Heman Sweatt Complex) with the promise of a new men's dormitory building in the near future.

The promise was fulfilled in the following decade when the university conceived an ambitious program to construct a group of men's residence halls southeast of the Forty Acres within a short walk of Gregory Gymnasium, the football stadium, and the baseball field. Some distance from the academic part of the campus and with plenty of nearby outlets for active male energies, this district had been designated as a location for men's dormitories in a master plan by James M. White as early as 1923.

Paul Cret's plan of 1933 proposed eight dormitory buildings arranged around loosely defined courtyards stretching from 19th Street (now Martin Luther King Boulevard) to 21st Street. He aligned the northern four buildings with the grid of the campus and the southern four with the grid of the city. The Men's Dormitory Group was the only site in the 1933 plan where the two grids were conjoined.

The first of the buildings to be constructed was located just to the east of the intersection of Lampasas Street (now Speedway) and 21st Street, and the building's long front face stretched along the latter thoroughfare. It was named in honor of George Washington Brackenridge.

By the time the university was ready to begin the second building a different direction for the site plan had emerged. Breaking with the 1933 plan, the new buildings were built to the east of Brackenridge Hall, rather than south toward 19th Street, thereby creating a stronger link between the academic campus and the football stadium. The addition of Roberts Hall in 1936, Prather Hall in 1937, Hill Hall in 1939, and Moore Hall in 1954 formed a cohesive ensemble of men's dormitories with 21st Street as its core. Though considerably varied in architectural character, the long, thin buildings create well-scaled, beautifully proportioned open spaces linked by gateways, loggias, and terraces.

72. Brackenridge Hall

Paul Cret, Consulting Architect; Herbert M. Greene, LaRoche and Dahl, 1932

Particularly notable as the earliest building on the campus with Paul Cret's name on the cornerstone, Brackenridge Hall documents a significant departure Cret initiated from previous buildings on campus. Whereas most of the buildings of the previous twenty years had symmetrical compositions, typically based on a palazzo format, Brackenridge Hall is markedly asymmetrical, with a long wing and a stepped back short wing linked by a vertical tower at their intersection.

The composition is more informal, picturesque, and rural in feeling than Gilbert's strong, urbane buildings and Greene's works that followed them. The materials

Brackenridge Hall

are rougher, the window patterns less regular, and the detailing looser. Though Brackenridge Hall seems an experimental building with many unresolved moments, it is clearly the precursor to a vocabulary Cret would use with great skill in later dormitories and, most notably, in the Architecture Building (now Goldsmith Hall) and the Texas Union. Compositions of various additive volumes of different heights and highly textured walls with irregular window patterns would become hallmarks of some of Cret's best work on the campus.

The primary building material, brick, is used in a variety of configurations and coursing types. The brick blend is lighter than that used by Gilbert and Greene, and the general face brick is laid very irregularly, with random bricks set out slightly from the face of the wall to give a highly textured feeling. Windows are placed singularly and in pairs, sometimes separated by a pier and sometimes combined to make a double unit reflecting the internal organization of the residential floors. The large size of the operable windows and their orientation to the prevailing breeze provided cooling ventilation in the days before air-conditioning, which was not installed until the 1990s.

The top floor of the dormitory features buff-colored stucco panels set into brick frames. At the center of each panel is a dark brown icon depicting masculine symbols of Texas and the Old West that range from firearms to ranching gear to a longhorn. Only the last of these seems even remotely germane to UT students today, but in the 1930s, many depression-era students from rural Texas would have found them familiar.

In contrast to the double-occupancy rooms, Murphy beds, and big closets of Littlefield Dormitory for women, Brackenridge Hall's male inhabitants lived in a more Spartan manner sleeping barrack-style in bunk beds packed into large rooms and porches (now enclosed). Slightly more privacy was available in the smaller study rooms in which each resident had a desk and a closet for his personal possessions.

73. Roberts Hall

Paul Cret, Consulting Architect; Robert Leon White, Architect, 1936

Although the general plan and massing of Roberts Hall is a near mirror image of Brackenridge Hall, it is a very different building in materials and detail. In the four years that ensued between the two buildings, Paul Cret had developed his own distinctive palette of materials and compositional vocabulary.

Though the brick is still laid irregularly, the color here is lighter and yellower than that of Brackenridge Hall. It no longer is the visually dominant material but serves as an infill between a strong limestone frame of base and cap linked by quoins at the corners. The ornament has been upgraded as well in terms of traditional motifs with images of rural life giving way to a lone star signifying Texas, and emblems of

Roberts Hall

learning: quill, book, and owl. A modest loggia with brick piers and heavy wood framing links Brackenridge and Roberts halls visually, though not functionally, and provides a gateway between 21st Street and the unrealized courtyard planned to the south.

Roberts Hall was named for Texas Governor Oran Milo Roberts, who led the state during the years encompassing the construction of the Capitol and the founding of the university. He also served as professor of law from 1883 to 1893.

74. Prather Hall
Paul Cret, Consulting Architect; Robert Leon White, Architect, 1937

Built only a year after Roberts Hall, Prather Hall follows the lead of its predecessor in massing, composition, material selection, and details. The primary differences between them stem from the fact that Prather runs parallel to the slope of the land whereas Roberts runs perpendicular to it, which required modest changes in plan configuration and floor levels. Thus, the entries at Prather face what was to become a courtyard rather than the street, giving the building its "off the beaten path" identity.

Together, Roberts Hall and Prather Hall created a beautifully composed facade for the dormitory group facing east to Waller Creek. Their flat-roofed volumes flanked

Prather Hall

by five-story towers frame an opening to the courtyard beyond. A vine-covered trellis was planned to link the buildings together and to shelter an overlook perched high above the creek. Sadly, this area is currently dominated by two recently installed steel fire stairs. Though necessary, their massive volume and utilitarian character detract significantly from the original grace of this carefully planned outdoor space.

The building is named for Colonel William Lambdin Prather, who had the unusual distinction of serving as both a regent and president of the university around the turn of the nineteenth to the twentieth century. He is most famous for his exhortation to students, "The eyes of Texas are upon you," which would later inspire the words for the university's school song.

75. Hill Hall
Paul Cret, Consulting Architect; Robert Leon White, Architect, 1939

Built to house male athletes, Hill Hall was set apart from the other men's dormitories well to the north of 21st Street with its front door originally facing Gregory Gymnasium. It was named for Dr. Homer Barksdale Hill, an Austin doctor who lived

near the campus and volunteered to provide medical services to the UT football team from 1893 until his death in 1923.

The architectural character of the building incorporates a striking juxtaposition of simple, clean, modern wings and a tower with the more traditional vocabulary of Brackenridge, Roberts, and Prather halls. The three-story wings have flat roofs and a completely regular rhythm of identical steel-sash windows that reflect the modular rooms within. In contrast, the four-story tower element has a more vertical expression. It is faced

Hill Hall

Moore Hall

by panels of stucco on the top floor and capped by a hipped, red tile roof. Hill Hall exemplifies Cret's commitment to diversity and variation in the architectural language of the campus.

76. Moore Hall

Mark Lemmon, Consulting Architect; Page Southerland Page, Associate Architect, 1954

Moore Hall, also built to house male athletes, extended the footprint of Hill Hall to 21st Street. Its principal wing parallels the street like Roberts Hall, which it faces. Two shorter wings extend northward from it, the longer of the two connecting to Hill Hall. A large cafeteria, known as Varsity Cafeteria because of its use by the athletes, was located at the west end of the dormitory and had its own entrance off 21st Street. This somewhat separate part of the building has been used for a variety of non-dormitory functions since it was closed as a cafeteria in the 1980s.

Moore Hall seems a natural extension and elaboration of Hill Hall. It is composed primarily of three- and four-story flat-roofed brick volumes punctuated by steel-sash windows with very regular sizes and spacing. Other elements of the material palette and the classically derived ornamentation, however, more closely resemble Roberts and Prather halls.

Moore Hall was named for Dean Victor Ivan Moore who served as Dean of Men and Student Life beginning in 1927. Moore Hall and Hill Hall have been known since the 1950s as Moore-Hill Hall since they shared, for many years, a common identity as the athletes' dorm and operate as a single unit.

77. San Jacinto Residence Hall
Lotti Krishan Short, Inc., 2000

This 866-bed dorm was the first student housing project completed on the campus since the Jester Center opened its doors thirty years earlier. It reflects the Pelli Campus Master Plan's instruction to substantially increase the number of students living on campus. Though Pelli's site plan had stretched the dormitory along Waller Creek, the final configuration became much more conventional and less responsive to the creek with two distinct wings—one running north/south and the other running east/west—joined by a central entry.

Built in an era when eighty-five percent of incoming UT students had never shared a bedroom and eighty percent had never shared a bath, San Jacinto Hall was built with considerably more attention to privacy than earlier dorms. The price tag that came with individually controlled thermostats, private baths, and other amenities was about twenty percent higher than other on-campus housing, giving the dorm a reputation of exclusivity that was reinforced by its creek side location and views that rival some of Austin's best hotels.

San Jacinto Residence Hall

Etter-Harbin Alumni Center

78. Etter-Harbin Alumni Center

*Jessen, Jessen, Millhouse and Greeven, Consulting Architect; Day and
Newman, Architects, 1965; extension: Charles W. Moore Associates
with Richard L. Dodge, Consulting Architects; Jessen, Inc., Architect,
led by Fred W. Day, Jr., 1987*

The slogan for the new Alumni Center when it originally opened proclaimed, "It's your home away from home." The building matched that sentiment. The 14,400-square-foot single-story structure was like a sprawling ranch-style house with gracious, homey rooms arranged around a courtyard. Its lot on the tree-lined banks of Waller Creek added an almost rural feeling.

Beautifully appointed and detailed, the building owed much to the distinguished residential work of O'Neil Ford and Harwell Hamilton Harris in Texas of the prior decade. Sandy-beige brick and rough-sawn western red cedar framing and siding gave a soft feeling to the uncompromisingly modern plan and massing. At the entry, two bronze-cast handles with a condensed "U" affixed to a "T" plate accented solid mahogany doors set in a wall of glass. Inside, beamed ceilings expressed their construction while supporting four large Mexican chandeliers. Modernity and tradition blended gracefully with a distinctive Texan flavor.

By the time the Ex-Students' Association decided to triple the size of its facilities in the 1980s, the live oaks that had lined the street were gone and the residential scale of the Center had been dwarfed by the addition of Bellmont Hall to Memorial

Stadium. Charles Moore, recently appointed to the O'Neil Ford Chair in the School of Architecture, was a particularly appropriate choice to design the expansion. He had made his reputation as a designer of modern houses offering warmth and wit, and in the latter stages of his career had become a master at putting together disparate parts—knitting, assembling, and hybridizing with abandon.

Moore took the 1960s building as a springboard for the addition, but leaped to a much larger scale both inside and outside. The former courtyard became a grand concourse covered by a steeply pitched roof enlivened by a series of giant umbrellas and lanterns. The whole building embraced the creek with decks and patios nestled into the rocks and trees.

The Alumni Center is named for ex-students who were instrumental in funding the two different construction phases. Lila B. Etter graduated in 1892 and left a substantial portion of her estate for the construction of the original building. Jack Harbin graduated in 1939 and became a Distinguished Alumnus as well as a President of the Ex-Students' Association. He made a substantial contribution to the construction of the building extension.

Just to the north of the Center is the Texas Cowboy Pavilion, dedicated in 2004 and designed by Miró-Rivera Architects. (Juan Miró is a professor in the School of Architecture.)

79. Liberal Arts Building
Overland Partners, 2012 (projected)

Completing a new ensemble of buildings on the East Mall, the Liberal Arts Building continues the process of narrowing and containing the mall space begun by the Jackson Geological Sciences Building and reinforced by the Student Activities Center. Its massing will help define a new gateway to the central campus, and its program will stretch the traditional Liberal Arts presence on the Forty Acres much farther to the east.

80. Student Activities Center
Overland Partners and WTW Architects, 2011

One of the last substantial infill sites on the central campus was designated for a concentration of student-oriented uses in 2006 after evaluation of several other potential locations. The site's adjacency to Gregory Gymnasium, the East Mall, and the proposed Speedway Mall as well as its proximity to significantly underserved undergraduate student populations in Engineering and Fine Arts made it ideal for these purposes.

After the selection of an architect that same year, a process involving students fleshed out programmatic and design ideas and established the organizational concept of creating two building volumes—one with its short end facing the East Mall and the other with its short end facing Speedway Mall. The connective tissue between them was planned as an open, glassy, interactive zone of informal student activity.

Though the solid building volumes wear fairly traditional UT campus garb, the connecting zone takes more liberties. Here, the structure skips and dodges among the mature trees on the site and plays against prominent landscape and art features.

WALK FIVE: SPORTS, SOCIAL WORK, AND NURSING

With its towering upper decks visible for miles and overbearing presence when viewed from close range at Speedway and 23rd Street, Darrell K. Royal – Texas Memorial Stadium is the epicenter of The University of Texas at Austin's intercollegiate athletics empire where football is king but the other competitive sports are taken very, very seriously. Less well known outside the university community is the Division of Recreational Sports, in existence since 1916, which annually attracts the participation of 90 percent of the student population, over 45,000 men and women. The buildings and playing fields for both institutions cluster in the southeastern area of campus on both sides of Waller Creek and engulf the School of Social Work Building, the former University Junior High School, which stands as a reminder of the area's earlier history as a residential neighborhood.

The stadium has been in place since 1924, but the other structures serving intercollegiate and recreational sports are products of two building campaigns, the first tied to the campus-wide building boom of the 1960s and 1970s, the second beginning thirty years later. With regard to planning, the sports facilities pose a challenge in the way they relate to daily life on campus. They are large objects that form a barrier between the central part of campus and its outlying areas east of I-35 and south of Martin Luther King, Jr. Drive along Red River Street where the School of Nursing is located.

Architecturally, a significant development in recent intercollegiate athletic facilities is the renovation of mid-twentieth-century buildings (Moncrief-Neuhaus Athletics Center, Disch-Falk Field) and the design of new structures (additions to Royal–Memorial Stadium, Myers Stadium, McCombs Field) to accord with the "retro" look made popular by Oriole Park at Camden Yards (1992) in Baltimore designed by HOK Sport. This image replaced the raw look of 1960s-era stadia that had inspired the west upper deck and Bellmont Hall at Memorial Stadium and Disch-Falk Field. Besides associating UT's facilities with current taste, the particular composition of the "retro" look, using materials and colors reminiscent of older buildings on campus, serves to foster a sense of campus identity and to reinforce the image of UT athletics as a brand.

Disch-Falk Field and McCombs Field are part of the university's controversial expansion east of I-35. To their north is a patchwork of parking lots and support buildings that give a backyard character that, understandably, makes residents of the neighborhoods to the east nervous. Lingering suspicions of the university's intentions coupled with issues of class, race, and power make future development of the area a delicate matter. The old redevelopment strategy of displacement must be replaced by an approach by which the university fosters an environment capable of supporting a diverse population. The University Interscholastic League Building on Manor Road designed by Cotera, Kolar, Negrete and completed in 1998 is a notable work that reinforces the urban fabric and accommodates a function that is community-related.

81. Darrell K. Royal–Texas Memorial Stadium

Herbert M. Greene and James M. White, dedicated 1924; north horseshoe: A. T. Granger, 1926; southern seating and enlargements to east and west grandstands: George L. Dahl, 1947; west side upper deck: Osborn Engineering Company, 1969; east side upper deck: 1998; renovations to west side upper deck and south grandstand: 2005–2009; north side reconstruction and upper deck: Heery International, 2009

L. Theo Bellmont Hall

Osborn-Papesh, Architect; Osborn Engineering Company with Lockwood, Andrews and Newman, Engineer, 1969

Moncrief-Neuhaus Athletic Center

O'Connell, Robertson and Grobe, Architect, 1986; renovated and expanded: Heery International, 2006–2009

Reese M. Rowling Hall

Heery International, 1998

Like colossal sentries in parade dress, four brick-clad towers mark the approach to the shrine of University of Texas football. The elaborate architectural flourishes and luxury accommodations of today's 100,119-seat stadium are a far cry from the roughly finished grandstands that were rushed to completion in time to seat the 13,000 fans who attended the inaugural game against Baylor University on November 8, 1924.

Difficult to imagine today, the site on the east side of Waller Creek was once a hilly, partially wooded area occasionally used during the day by surveying classes and at night by amorous couples. The east grandstand was built into the rising slope. A bridge at 23rd Street provided access to the rest of the campus, but for years football players picked their way across the creek downstream as they moved between the locker room in the stadium and the practice field located on the site of the Jester Center. San Jacinto Boulevard was built in 1928.

Throughout most of its history, the stadium has been a work in progress. Little original fabric remains visible, and even the field has been lowered (1999) as well as having had a variety of natural and artificial playing surfaces over the years. The expansion completed in 2009 made an effort to connect modern fans to the stadium's early history. At the corner of San Jacinto and 23rd Street is a 47-foot-long bronze monument designed by S. C. P. Vosper and sculpted by Hugo Villia consisting of a female figure holding an olive branch and a tablet listing the 5,246 Texans known to have lost their lives in World War I. Originally installed in the north horseshoe in 1931, it was the centerpiece of the stadium's identification as a

L. Theo Bellmont Hall

World War I memorial. In 1997, the university expanded the scope of the memorial to include all students and alumni who have died in military service. The name of Darrell K. Royal, the football coach and athletic director who led the Longhorns to their first three national championships, was added to the stadium's dedication in 1996.

The construction of the west upper deck, completed in 1972, occasioned the cavernous L. Theo Bellmont Hall, which contains classrooms, offices, and sports facilities. Bellmont was a pioneering director of athletics in the early twentieth century who inaugurated many varsity and recreational sports programs and spearheaded the construction of the stadium. The size of the building cast the alumni center in deep shadow and required the displacement of San Jacinto Boulevard towards Waller Creek and the removal of more than two dozen trees. Student protests and a showdown with Frank Erwin, chairman

Moncrief-Neuhaus Athletic Center

Reese M. Rowling Hall

of the Board of Regents, in October 1969, led to the infamous "Battle of Waller Creek," arrests, and much ill will.

Less confrontational is the Moncrief-Neuhaus Athletic Center appended to the south side of the stadium. Honoring alumnus and philanthropist W. A. "Tex" Moncrief, Jr., and Vernon F. "Doc" Neuhaus, long-time member of the Intercollegiate Athletic Council for Men, it is the inner sanctum of the football program, housing locker rooms, training facilities, and coaches' offices. The roof serves as a half-size practice field.

Reese M. Rowling Hall, incorporated into the east upper deck, contains a gallery devoted to the history of Bevo, the university's longhorn mascot, as well as dining rooms of The University of Texas Club, skyboxes overlooking the field, and athletic department offices. Rowling was a successful oilman and generous supporter of the university. The Red McCombs Red Zone at the north end of the stadium makes an effort to engage daily life on campus with a food court and also contains the museum and library of the H. J. Lutcher Stark Center for Physical Culture and Sports.

82. Recreational Sports Center
Fisher & Spillman, 1990

UT was one of the first large universities to foresee the role athletics could play in fostering student socialization. Much more than just a gym, Recreational Sports was

Recreational Sports Center

planned to be a place for people to meet and congregate in an informal way. The building is equipped not only with aerobic rooms, weight training rooms, racquetball courts, and a large gymnasium that can accommodate three basketball courts, but also spaces for table tennis and martial arts, game rooms, and lounge areas with big-screen TVs. All of these use-specific spaces are glued together by wide, light-filled concourses and passageways that encourage casual encounters. The facility was a hit with students from opening day. In its first three weeks, over thirty thousand users passed through its doors, demonstrating the pent-up demand for such a sports/social center on campus.

83. School of Social Work Building

Paul Cret, Consulting Architect; Herbert M. Greene, LaRoche and Dahl, Architect, 1933

Originally built as the University High School, a junior high accommodating eight hundred students, this modest structure sat apart from rest of the campus serving as a bridge between town and gown. The facility was constructed by the university but was operated by the City of Austin as a model school and as a laboratory for the School of Education.

The layout for the building was a familiar one for progressive schools in the 1930s. Wide double-loaded corridors with classrooms on either side created interlocking wings that wrapped around three sides of a central courtyard. The fourth side was a deep shady loggia. As on so many other campus sites, the design of this sprawling structure had to respond to sloping terrain. Thus, the west face is mostly three stories while the east side nestles into the hill and becomes one or two stories. The main floor occupies the full building footprint, but the upper and lower floors are smaller.

The exterior of the building represents an economy version of the familiar campus architectural language. The base is board-formed concrete rather than stone, and the ornament is mostly limited to brick patterns, recalling other buildings of utilitarian character like Gregory Gymnasium and Hill Hall.

School of Social Work Building

Lee and Joe Jamail Texas Swimming Center

By the late 1960s the building was no longer used as a school and became a target for the wrecking ball when a 200,000-square-foot office building and a new Longhorn Band Hall were planned for the site. It escaped destruction but remained somewhat derelict and underutilized until 1994 when it was modestly refurbished for use by the School of Social Work.

84. Lee and Joe Jamail Texas Swimming Center
Fisher & Spillman, 1977; renovated: 2001

Mute, tan-brick walls recalling the austere forms of Fisher & Spillman's contemporary Fine Arts Complex encase the theatrical setting of the Texas Swimming Center's 50-meter pool, diving well, and 2,000-seat grandstand. The Center is named for philanthropists Lee and Joe Jamail who have received distinguished alumnus awards for their service to the university and accomplishments in their respective professions of speech pathology and law.

Across the street from the swimming center is the reconstructed pumpjack of Santa Rita No. 1, an artifact of pivotal importance to campus architecture. Santa Rita No. 1 was the well on university land in Reagan County that on May 28, 1923, struck oil and transformed sixty-four square miles of grazing land into the site of lucrative oil leases. The income made the building campaigns of the late 1920s and 1930s possible and provides the basis for much of the endowment supporting public higher education in Texas today. History professor Walter Prescott Webb and engineering professor Carl Eckhardt led the effort to bring to Austin historic components of the well, which were installed on this site in 1958.

85. Collections Deposit Library

Brooks, Barr, Graeber and White, Consulting Architect; Fred W. Day, Associate Architect, 1966

Collections Deposit Library

Variously known as the "mushroom" or "fortress," the Collections Deposit Library provides the University Libraries with convenient off-site storage for little-used books and periodicals. The reinforced-concrete piers and cantilevered beams along the perimeter express the structural system while panels of Cordova Shell limestone and the tiled roof refer to older campus buildings. In contrast to the squat exterior, the interior contains six levels, three of which are underground.

86. Nursing School and Centennial Park

Simpson and Lackey, 1971

Completed in 1973, the Nursing School is the best example on campus of New Brutalism, an architectural style widely employed for university and civic buildings for a brief time in the late 1960s and early 1970s. Hallmarks of the style include exposed reinforced-concrete structural elements, sun-screening fins (Le Corbusier's *brises soleils*), and the raising of portions of the building above ground level with slender columns (*pilotis*). All appear in the Nursing School and may be seen to best advantage on the south façade. The building has a rectangular plan arranged around a large courtyard that once extended through a breezeway beneath the west wing (now enclosed) to a terrace that offers magnificent views of Waller Creek and the State Capitol complex beyond.

To the south of the Nursing School is Centennial Park, a project of the Austin Chamber of Commerce to mark the university's centennial in 1983. Designed by landscape architect Stephen K. Domigan, it features a path that winds among low mounds and shade trees past the bronze "Three Muses" by Charles Umlauf

Nursing School and Centennial Park

(originally displayed in the Flawn Academic Center), to a cylindrical time capsule. The paving tiles bear the names of the thousands of people who donated money for the park.

87. Frank C. Erwin Jr. Special Events Center
B. W. Wilson and Ralph Anderson of Wilson Crain & Anderson, Architect, 1977; renovations: Heery International, 2001–2003

Denton A. Cooley Pavilion
Heery International, 2005

Big and brash, "The Drum" dominates its hilltop site without a trace of the street grid and residential neighborhood it replaced as part of the Brackenridge Urban Redevelopment Project. Named for regent Frank C. Erwin Jr. who engineered the explosive growth of the university's physical plant from 1963 to 1975, the 16,734-seat arena accommodates basketball games and a variety of other events including rock concerts and high school commencement ceremonies. Modifications to the interior in 2003 added luxury suites and upgraded public services on the concourses. The Cooley Pavilion next door, named for Dr. Denton A. Cooley, former basketball letterman and surgeon who performed the first successful heart transplant in the U.S., provides practice courts and locker and training rooms for the men's and women's basketball teams.

Frank C. Erwin Jr. Special Events Center

The Erwin Center's architect, Wilson Crain & Anderson, was the designer of the "eighth wonder of the world," the Houston Astrodome (1965). The Drum, standing like a dramatic, isolated object approached by broad ramps, seems like a diminutive distant cousin of the Dome. Its design approach requires more open space than the tightly bounded site provides, and the result is particularly harsh along Red River Street where the edge of its plinth overwhelms the sidewalk and the afternoon sun turns the unshaded ramps into reflector ovens.

Arno Nowotny Building

88. Arno Nowotny Building
Abner Cook, 1857

John W. Hargis Hall
Middle section, 1888; north section: Ayres and Boyce, 1891; south section: J. L. O'Connor, 1900

In 1987, the Board of Regents named the park-like site bounded by Martin Luther King Jr. Boulevard, Red River Street, the Erwin Special Events Center, and the I-35 frontage road the Heman Sweatt Campus in honor of Heman Marion Sweatt, whose landmark case heard by the United States Supreme Court in 1950 paved the way for the desegregation of the university's graduate and professional schools. The regents also dedicated one of the two buildings on the site to another pioneering African American student, John W. Hargis, who earned a bachelor's degree in chemical engineering in 1959. This recognition of the men and women who courageously asserted their rightful places on campus was a component of an effort to define the Sweatt Campus as the university's front door, and, indeed, many undergraduates have begun their UT experience with a visit to the Freshman Admissions Center in Hargis Hall.

Despite the official attention, the site has an awkward relationship with its immediate surroundings that makes it anomalous: it is hemmed in by busy streets and the interstate highway, the oddly spaced buildings face south and away from the rest of the campus, and there is an abrupt change of scale from the park to the

John W. Hargis Hall

monolithic mass of the Erwin Center. These discrepancies are clues to the site's rich history that begins decades before the building of the Forty Acres and weaves through the not always aligned interests of city, state, and university.

What is now the Arno Nowotny Building was realized by Austin builder Abner Cook, who is best known for his Greek Revival houses, including the Governor's Mansion (1856). The two-story Italianate structure was the first building of the Texas Asylum for the Blind, one of the state's early public service agencies. It occupied the crest of the ridge above Waller Creek and faced south towards the city. Following the Civil War, the institution was temporarily displaced for use as the headquarters and residence of General George Armstrong Custer who commanded a federal occupation force in 1865. Although Custer's stay was less than a year, his association with the building would become a rallying point for its preservation in the 1970s.

Over the next fifty years, the institute for the blind grew from a single building to a campus of dormitories, classrooms, and workshops loosely grouped around a courtyard landscaped with a variety of trees, grass, and shrubs. The three units of Hargis Hall, known then as Building H, framed the west side of the courtyard. In 1917, the Texas School for the Blind, as it was then known, moved to a larger site elsewhere in Austin, and the state transferred the management of these facilities to the university. Around this time it acquired the name Little Campus, which remains in common usage today.

For decades the Little Campus functioned as overflow space for student housing and various academic and administrative programs. From the 1930s to 1962, generations of male students occupying its low-cost accommodations maintained a tightly knit, often boisterous community in the spirit of B Hall on the Forty Acres. While useful, the Little Campus buildings had no architectural relationship to the rest of the campus, and the university envisioned their eventual replacement. That opportunity arrived in 1967 with the acquisition of the adjacent Brackenridge urban redevelopment tract. The regents subsequently voted to demolish the complex, but their plans ran into an obstacle when the Texas Antiquities Committee declared the site to be a state archeological landmark and the Nowotny Building was listed on the National Register of Historic Places.

Throughout most of the 1970s, the university demolished what it could while contesting the Antiquities Committee's jurisdiction and fighting losing battles with a grassroots protest led by graduate student Susan Barry, the Austin Historic Landmarks Commission, and influential former residents of the men's dormitory including Congressman J. J. "Jake" Pickle and Houston attorney Percy Foreman. In 1978, the regents agreed to preserve the Nowotny Building and Hargis Hall, the only buildings remaining on the site.

Handsome as it appears today, the Nowotny Building is not the structure known to most of the residents of the School for the Blind or the UT dormitory. In the years following its use by Custer, it had been transformed by the addition of a third floor, a three-level front porch, and a two-story wing to the west. The combination of Custer's aura and the local significance of the original builder, however, offered justification to remove the layers of history and restore the building as an artifact of the 1860s.

89. UFCU Disch-Falk Field

Marmon Mok, 1975; renovation: DLR Group in association with O'Connell Robertson & Associates, 2008

UFCU Disch-Falk Field is the university's third baseball park. The first, established in 1897 on the site of the present A.C.E.S. Building at 24th Street and Speedway, accommodated football as well as baseball and was named Clark Field in honor

of respected early administrator and regent James Benjamin Clark. The name was
retained for the second park, which stood from 1928 to 1974 on a site north of
Memorial Stadium now occupied by the Performing Arts Center, but the present
field is dedicated to former baseball coaches Billy Disch and Bibb Falk. The local
University Federal Credit Union, a generous benefactor, added its name to the
marquee in 2006.

The construction of the Performing Arts Center was not the only impetus for the
replacement of the second Clark Field. Another issue was the park's idiosyncratic
right field, which included a twelve-foot limestone cliff known as Billy Goat Hill
within fair territory. It gave a decidedly home-field advantage to UT outfielders who
knew the quickest ways up the slope but also posed a collision hazard to players
of both teams.

The new ballpark provided a level playing field in more ways than one. It
was designed to conform to the contemporary practice in major league parks of

UFCU Disch–Falk Field

emphasizing symmetry in the layout of left and right fields. It also followed the trend of covering the field with Astroturf rather than natural grass, a practice popularized by the use of the material in the Houston Astrodome in 1966. Since 2008, the surface has been Fieldturf, another synthetic material.

DLR's renovation wrapped the 1975 grandstand with a brick, metal, and glass facade intended to complement the monumental character of the nearby Red and Charline McCombs Field for softball, Memorial Stadium, and other recent sports venues. The addition expanded seating to over 6,500, increased areas for concessions and rest rooms, and provided new locker rooms and training facilities.

90. Red and Charline McCombs Field
Marmon Mok, 2008

A grand portal conducts spectators to a veritable field of dreams with lush grass and a perfectly groomed clay infield. Seating 1,200, McCombs Field is home to the Longhorn softball team and is named for alumnus and businessman Red McCombs and his wife, Charline, generous supporters of the university and other philanthropies throughout Texas.

Red and Charline McCombs Field

Mike A. Myers Track and Soccer Stadium

91. Mike A. Myers Track and Soccer Stadium
John S. Chase Architects, Inc., 2000

Named for philanthropic alumnus and businessman Mike A. Myers, the Track
and Soccer Stadium was designed by architect John S. Chase, a pioneer in the
desegregation of the university and the profession of architecture in Texas. Chase
was one of the first African Americans to enroll in the university, the first African
American to graduate from the School of Architecture, and the first African American
to practice as a registered architect in Texas. The Track and Soccer Stadium was his
second university commission. The first was a large parking garage at 25th and San
Antonio streets (1992).

WALK SIX: FINE ARTS, TEXAS MEMORIAL MUSEUM, LAW, AND THE LBJ COMPLEX

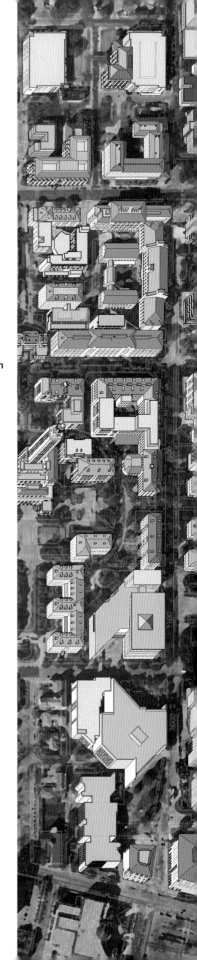

The topography of the eastern portion of campus from Winship Drama Building at the base of the East Mall to Sid Richardson Hall up the hill at Red River Street is among the most varied on campus, even though many of the natural contours have been reshaped in the course of constructing buildings and roads. From the terrace alongside Winship, steps lead down to the bed of a shady stretch of Waller Creek where one can occasionally see a Great Blue Heron fishing for minnows. Across San Jacinto Boulevard, which was not laid out until 1928, the land rises. The slope ascends somewhat steeply opposite 24th Street to a ridge, which Paul Cret envisioned as an acropolis crowned by the Texas Memorial Museum (1936). Eighteen years later, Mark Lemmon added the new home of the Law School, Townes Hall.

In the early twentieth century, the land bounded by Waller Creek, Robert Dedman Drive, 24th Street, and Dean Keeton Street belonged to Texas Wesleyan College, run by Swedish Methodists. The college erected a building in 1911, approximately where Jesse H. Jones Hall stands now. The University of Texas at Austin acquired the property in 1931, and during World War II, the Wesleyan College building became the Defense Research Laboratory. After the war temporary housing was built on the sites occupied today by Townes Hall, the Connally Center, and the Butler School of Music buildings.

East of Robert Dedman Drive, family homes and boarding houses lined a regular grid of streets. The university's acquisition of land in 1965 for the construction of the LBJ complex inaugurated the clearing of the entire area, so all that remains of the neighborhood today is the short stretch of Clyde Littlefield Drive, which retains its original alignment.

The combination of varied terrain, the university's "clean slate" approach to development, and mid-twentieth-century taste for buildings viewed as free-standing objects or isolated groups conspired to give this portion of campus more the character of a suburban office park than the dense, urban structure of the Forty Acres. With its stadiums, art gallery and museums, theaters, concert halls, renowned research libraries, and ready access to major traffic arteries, the area has become the principal point of entry to the university for thousands of visitors. Its full significance as a portal has yet to be realized architecturally.

92. F. Loren Winship Drama Building

Jessen, Jessen, Millhouse and Greeven, Consulting Architects;
Bartlett Cocke, Associate Architect, 1960; addition and renovation:
Fisher & Spillman, 1974

Laboratory Theater Building

Page Southerland Page, 1959

The Department of Drama (now Department of Theater and Dance) inhabited makeshift quarters in the former Woman's Building near the Texas Union for nineteen years until a fire destroyed the structure in January 1959. By September, the Laboratory Theater Building opened on a site previously occupied by World War II–era barracks near the future East Mall. Today it is hidden behind the Jackson Geological Sciences Building. The awkward location reflects the unsettled plans for the mall and the adjacent Drama Building as the role of Consulting Architect passed from Page Southerland Page, who designed the Laboratory Theater, to Jessen, Jessen, Millhouse and Greeven, who had responsibility for the remainder of the complex.

Budgetary concerns split the design of the Drama Building into two phases. The first, alongside Waller Creek, was completed in 1962. It contains classrooms, rehearsal spaces, offices, shops, and a 200-seat experimental theater named for longtime faculty member Oscar G. Brockett. The second phase containing a proscenium theater was delayed more than a decade, and in the interim, the scope of work changed. Seating in the theater, which is named for Shakespearean actor and faculty member B. Iden Payne, was reduced by half to five hundred, and the entire building was extended to align more closely with the Jackson Building and the mall. A trace of the original entrance survives in the sky-lit atrium in the lobby of the Brockett Theater.

The additions conformed the appearance of the Winship Building with the favored look for campus buildings in the late 1960s and 1970s: crisply defined massing, large expanses of brick, and deeply set openings. In contrast, the remnants

of Jessen, Jessen, Millhouse and Greeven's architecture on the north and east sides are less monumental and employ materials inspired by earlier campus buildings: panels of warm-hued brick, bands of limestone marking the structural bays, and a thin water table of granite.

F. Loren Winship, for whom the building is named, was a pioneering

F. Loren Winship Drama Building

Art Building

chairman of the Department of Theater and Dance and was involved with drama at UT from 1928 to 1973.

93. Art Building
Page Southerland Page, Associate Architect; Brooks and Barr, Project Architect, 1961; addition and renovation: Fisher & Spillman, 1974; Visual Arts Center: Lake | Flato Architects, Inc., 2009

The Art Building is where UT's architects began their twenty-year love affair with vast expanses of brick and austere, geometric massing. The grand staircase along San Jacinto Boulevard and the shear wall towering above it have a monumental effect but offer no indication of the creative life within. The recent renovation by Lake | Flato Architects addresses this condition by adding a welcoming entrance oriented toward the Doty Fine Arts Building and cutting openings in the south and east facades with views into the new Visual Arts Center, which occupies space formerly devoted to the university's first art museum.

The 1974 addition stands to the north of the original building and is recognized easily by the brown brick on its exterior, the uniform of the campus's fine arts buildings in the mid-1970s. It doubled the size of the Art Building and helped relieve crowding from enrollment that had tripled since 1960. The architecture is bland, but terraces on the north side equipped with kilns and areas for metalwork are full of life.

Fine Arts Complex

94. E. William Doty Fine Arts Building
Fisher and Spillman Architects, 1979

95. Nancy Lee and Perry R. Bass Concert Hall
Fisher and Spillman Architects, 1981; renovation:
BOORA Architects, 2009

96. McCullough Theater & Drama Workshops
Fisher and Spillman Architects, 1980

97. Music Building East
Brooks, Barr, Graeber and White, Consulting Architect;
Marmon and Mok, Associate Architect, 1968

98. Music Building and Recital Hall
Fisher and Spillman Architects, 1976

When the Department of Music moved into Homer Rainey Hall in 1942, it seemed likely that the other units of the College of Fine Arts would follow and build on the southwest quadrant of the Forty Acres. The sharp enrollment increases after World War II, however, required larger facilities than the site could accommodate, so Dean Doty looked to the less congested east side of campus near San Jacinto Boulevard. This area offered an additional advantage in its emerging role as an interface between town and gown. The theaters, lecture halls, and art museum of the departments of Drama and Art soon complemented this program. A building for the Department of Music followed eight years later.

In 1972, the Board of Regents announced its intention to complete the consolidation of the college by constructing a performing arts center, which would be the largest single building project the university had undertaken. The Dallas architecture firm of Fisher & Spillman proceeded rapidly with preliminary plans, which included additions to the Winship Building and the Art Building, but problems with funding delayed construction of the new buildings for five years. The complex was dedicated in April 1981.

Music Building and Recital Hall

The stark, imposing forms of the brick buildings are tempered by the soft curves of the landscape with its stands of trees and a swale that winds along the west side of the Doty Building. Two features of significance to campus history may be seen at the eastern edge of the plaza facing Bass Concert Hall. The eleven-bell chime, donated to the university in 1929 by Albert Sidney Burleson, originally hung in the tower of Old Main Building. The grassy rise leading to Robert Dedman Drive is a trace of Billy Goat Hill, a limestone outcrop that ran across a portion of Clark Field, the university's baseball park before Disch-Falk Field.

Honoring philanthropists Nancy Lee and Perry R. Bass, the Concert Hall houses a 2,900-seat theater. The renovation by BOORA Architects expanded the

Nancy Lee and Perry R. Bass Concert Hall

E. William Doty Fine Arts Building

lobbies toward the plaza and made them visible by replacing the brick facade with a glass curtain wall. The adjacent E. William Doty Fine Arts Building is named for the college's vibrant first dean. It houses the Fine Arts Library, which has a double-height reading room and reference area lined with windows that achieves, spatially, something of the inspiring grandeur of the Battle Hall reading room.

The plaza facing Bass Concert Hall unequivocally announces the public entrance to the building, but the entrances to the two other major performance halls in the complex are less obvious. That of the 400-seat Ralph and Ruth McCullough Theater, which abuts the Drama Workshops behind the Concert Hall, seems almost an afterthought. The 700-seat Kate Broocks Bates Recital Hall, honoring a philanthropic Houston family, is tucked within the labyrinthine and imposing spaces of the Music Building and Recital Hall. The effort required to find the hall is well rewarded by the intimacy of the space and the presence of the visually and acoustically spectacular Visser-Rowland tracker pipe organ.

99. Texas Memorial Museum
Paul Cret, Consulting Architect; John F. Staub, Architect; 1936

If the Texas Memorial Museum looks more like a memorial than a museum, it is because the existing building is only a fragment of the ambitious structure Paul Cret and Houston architect John F. Staub planned for the site. Absent are large, flanking wings that would have contained the primary galleries and exhibit preparation areas. Repeated efforts to secure funding for their construction in the 1940s and 1950s failed, and the land required for the expansion was assigned other purposes. Throughout the museum's history, the staff has struggled to present its rich collections of natural and human history in the modest galleries surrounding Memorial Hall, the great room that Cret and Staub had intended as a solemn space in which visitors would pause to contemplate the "heroic period of early Texas history."

The idea of establishing a state museum at the university had been promoted vigorously in the 1920s by science faculty led by J. E. Pearce, Professor of Anthropology, but funds did not become available until it was tied to the Texas Centennial, celebrated in 1936. Special appropriations by the United States Congress and the Texas Legislature augmented proceeds from the sale of commemorative half dollars by the American Legion. Initially operated as an independent state entity, the museum was placed under the authority of the university by the legislature in 1959.

The building exemplifies Paul Cret's "New Classicism," which observed the principles of classical composition but simplified massing and detailing to emphasize tectonic clarity and volume. These qualities are evident on the monumental west facade in the symmetry of the composition, the fluted pilaster strips and classical

Texas Memorial Museum

moldings, the homogeneity of the Cordova Shell and Cordova Cream limestone cladding, and the tall, glass-block windows that express the Memorial Hall within. Dedicatory inscriptions and bas-reliefs proclaim the building's noble purpose. Overall, it has a striking familial resemblance to Cret's contemporary Folger Shakespeare Library in Washington, D.C.

A series of terraces and a lawn descend the hill to San Jacinto Boulevard and the bronze statuary group, "The Mustangs," dedicated in 1948. Funded by Ralph R. Ogden, an Austin businessman, it is the work of sculptor A. Phimister Proctor. J. Frank Dobie composed the inscriptions celebrating the role of mustangs in the settlement of the West.

Law School

100. Townes Hall
Mark Lemmon, Architect, 1952; additions: Mark Lemmon with Jessen, Jessen, Millhouse and Greeven, 1964; remodeling: Jessen Associates, Inc., 1980; remodeling of classrooms and dining areas: Susman Tisdale Gayle Architects, 2006

101. Jesse H. Jones Hall
Jessen Associates, Inc., 1980

102. John B. Connally Center for the Administration of Justice
3D/International, Inc., 1997

Townes Hall

Jesse H. Jones Hall

The three buildings housing the Law School seem remote from the rest of campus even though the Music Building is directly across Trinity Street. This sense of isolation was even more acute when Townes Hall opened in 1953. The new building replaced a cluster of temporary housing units known as Oak Grove Court, and the nearest building of note was the Texas Memorial Museum. Immediately to the west was the fenced compound of the U.S. Navy's Defense Research Laboratory. Down the slope to the north were the backyards of houses facing Park Place, since replaced by the much wider Dean Keeton Street, and to the east was the old alignment of Red River Street, loosely corresponding to Robert Dedman Street today. Despite its distance from other academic buildings and the commercial attractions of Guadalupe Street, the hilltop location with its grove of live oak trees provided room for Dean Page Keeton to realize his dream of a nationally prominent legal studies center with a major library, continuing education programs, dormitory housing for law students, and plenty of parking.

Townes Hall, named for former Law School dean John Charles Townes, was the first phase of the enterprise. It consisted of three distinct blocks. The westernmost unit, entered through a broad, recessed portal bearing the inscription, "That they

John B. Connally Center for the Administration of Justice

may truly and impartially administer justice," taken from the Anglican and Episcopalian Book of Common Prayer, contained a 750-seat auditorium (now the Charles I. Francis Auditorium). Classrooms, study areas, offices, and a faculty library occupied the central unit. The majority of the eastern unit was devoted to the Tarlton Library. Townes Hall employs a fine-grain Indiana limestone, similar to that of Main Building, rather than the local Cordova stone used elsewhere on the campus. The ornament of Townes Hall invokes the Spanish colonial architecture of the Forty Acres, though in a markedly dour iteration.

Within a decade, the once generous facilities had become overcrowded. Although Mark Lemmon no longer served as Consulting Architect, the university once again retained him, along with Jessen, Jessen, Millhouse and Greeven, to design additions to the north of the auditorium and library wings. A loggia between them encloses a small courtyard. This expansion proved to be only a stopgap solution. By the mid-1970s, competition among the 1,500 students for the library's 300 seats had become heated.

Jesse H. Jones Hall, dedicated in 1981, more than doubled the size of the Law School's facilities. It is the second building on campus honoring the philanthropy of the Houston businessman and civic leader. Most of the massive, box-like structure is occupied by the Joseph D. Jamail Legal Research Center, which includes the Tarlton Library, relocated from the east wing of Townes Hall.

The center honoring Governor John B. Connally is devoted to the research and practice of conflict resolution. It stands immediately to the south of the east wing of Townes Hall, and the windows of the former library reading room now look into a slender atrium that separates the two buildings. 3D/International matched the limestone, cornices, and red tile roof of the older building but differentiated their work by taking a more severe approach to the fenestration, punching openings rather than surrounding them with ornamental frames.

103. Creekside Residence Hall

Mark Lemmon, Consulting Architect; Wilson, Morris & Crain, Architect, 1954

After World War II, the university erected five military surplus barracks to serve as dormitories on the east side of San Jacinto Boulevard approximately where the parking garage (1986) stands today. The utilitarian structures contrasted sharply with

Creekside Residence Hall

the rustic character of the grove of trees along Waller Creek. In 1952, the distance from other dormitories and the spare accommodations were factors in the decision to open some units to the university's first male African American graduate students.

The patience of the residents, black and white, must have been severely tested as they watched the new, air-conditioned dormitory for white graduate and law students rise outside their doorsteps in 1954. No less galling was the building's dedication to William Stewart Simkins, professor of law from 1899 to 1929 who, before coming to Texas, had organized the Ku Klux Klan in Florida. The dormitory did not become available to African Americans until the regents integrated all university housing in 1964. Its name was changed to Creekside in 2010.

Creekside Hall is a two-story brick structure with a red tile roof. The T-shaped plan was designed to interlock with a second unit, unrealized, forming a courtyard. The setback along the west facade was to have framed a terrace and a walkway that would have extended across the creek to the Home Economics Teahouse that once stood near the present intersection of San Jacinto and Dean Keeton.

104. J. Frank Dobie House
C. H. Toungate, Builder, 1925; extension: Carlton Brush, Architect, 1950

Folklorist and man of letters J. Frank Dobie and his wife, Bertha, purchased this modest colonial revival house in 1926. It was here that he wrote many of the novels,

J. Frank Dobie House

Joe C. Thompson Conference Center

short stories, and essays that brought national recognition to the literature of Texas and the Southwest. Until his death in 1964, Dobie presided over an informal seminar of faculty, students, and visitors that met under an elm in the backyard overlooking Waller Creek. The acquisition of the home by the university in 1995 enabled literary discussions to continue under the auspices of the James A. Michener Center for Writers.

105. Joe C. Thompson Conference Center
Fisher & Spillman, 1970

The two-and-one-half acre site at the northeast corner of the campus was acquired as part of University East Urban Renewal Project in 1968. It offered ample room for a planned but never realized expansion of the conference center, which houses meeting rooms of various sizes and a 300-seat auditorium in a boxy mass faced mostly in Cordova Shell Limestone with tiny vertical slit windows.

There are some lovely site-responsive moves in the lower part of the building—a shady, intimate court around a shapely live oak on the north side and graceful terracing of the building as the land slopes to the west. Within, a single-story mass in the center steps down to a double height dining room that affords pleasant views but takes a beating by the afternoon sun despite the presence of vertical concrete sunshades.

106. Lyndon Baines Johnson Library and Museum
Gordon Bunshaft of Skidmore, Owings & Merrill with Brooks, Barr, Graeber and White, dedicated 1971; renovations: Overland Partners, 2009

Ada Louise Huxtable, the foremost architectural critic of her generation, noted shortly after the completion of the LBJ Library that the building marked the beginning of a new era in American monument building. "The age of Lincoln and Jefferson Memorials is over," she wrote. "It will be presidential libraries from now on." She admired the boldness and strength of the building, observing, "In the random way that democracy scatters art and monuments among its leaders, Johnson has a winner."

Only the sixth presidential library to be built and the first to be located on a university campus, the LBJ Library set the bar for this new building type. As Huxtable noted at the time, "The Johnson Library is big—Texas big. The architect, Gordon Bunshaft, thinks big. Johnson is known not to think small." Almost three decades after its completion, the LBJ Library still records the highest overall visitation of any of the fifteen presidential libraries outside of initial years of operation.

Lyndon Baines Johnson Library and Museum

Dramatically sited on the high point of a thirteen-acre site that includes a magnificent fountain, the building has a dominant presence with long vistas to it from all sides. It even holds its own against the gargantuan Darrell K. Royal-Texas Memorial Stadium downhill to the southwest. The library's solid, un-ornamented, and unpunctuated east and west walls, two hundred feet long and sixty-five feet high, are faced in travertine and have the scale of a monument from an ancient civilization.

The tenth-floor mass that spans the ninety feet between them and cantilevers sixteen feet more on either side establishes an elemental clarity for the building that is simple and timeless while also being uncompromisingly modern.

The details of the building's exterior are visually refined and sophisticated. The gentle curve of the flanking walls, the pin connections and glass slots that form the junction between the top floor and the walls, and the metal caps on the post-tensioned girders all help elucidate the structural role of each of the building's components. The paired nature of the girders give a powerful rhythm to the deep soffit that is not unlike what can be observed on many other campus buildings from the 1918 Sutton Hall to a closer contemporary, the Flawn Academic Center, built in 1963.

Gordon Bunshaft was one of the foremost architects of his era. He won the Pritzker Prize in 1988. Though less has been written about him than some of his contemporaries like Louis Kahn and Phillip Johnson (both of whom were considered by President and Mrs. Johnson for the commission), his buildings have stood the test of time remarkably well. Among them are Lever House (1952) in New York City, Yale University's Beinecke Rare Books Library (1960–1963), and the Hirshhorn Museum (1974) on the Mall in Washington, D.C. It was Lady Bird Johnson's visit to the Beinecke Library in the fall of 1965 that put Bunshaft on the short list of architects under consideration. She liked the fact that in the Beinecke "the outside is cold and severe, and you walk inside and it's very warm and rich." She also felt that the selected architect should be able to "work well with the university's own firm of Brooks, Barr [Graeber and White]." Bunshaft may have had an inside track on that account since he had been a student at MIT with Max Brooks.

Standing in the Great Hall at the north end of the building's interior, a debt to the Beinecke Library is certainly clear. The five-story, glass-encased view of 4,200 flag-red buckram manuscript boxes is reminiscent of the dramatic illuminated rare books cube at the center of the Yale library. But the spatial volume, the grand staircase, the gently curving travertine walls, and the deep coffered ceiling in the Great Hall set it apart from any direct precedent.

A recording in the library's archive of a telephone conversation between President Johnson and Gordon Bunshaft documents the history of another much-visited interior space in the LBJ Library. The call was made while the building was under construction, and the president is conveying to his very nervous architect an idea that has just occurred to him: adding a full-scale reproduction of the Oval Office as it was during the Johnson presidency. Bunshaft timidly resists but, ultimately, assures the persistent president that it can be done. In the end, structural limitations precluded a full-scale reproduction, and a 7/8-scale version was squeezed awkwardly into the top floor at the south end of the building. Despite having the slightly unsettling effect of a fun-house mirror and facade, it is charming, evocative, and popular with visitors.

Sid Richardson Hall

The recent renovations by Overland Partners and Hargreaves Associates landscape architects addressed long-standing technical problems largely due to years of unchecked water penetration through the building's skin and the surface of the plaza, beneath which is a 1,000-seat auditorium as well as other educational functions. The original travertine and terrazzo paving was replaced with two different colors of granite that keep a sense of the original hues. The plaza to the east of the library, barren following an earlier renovation that removed leaking fountains, has been softened by a garden dedicated to Lady Bird Johnson.

107. Sid Richardson Hall

Gordon Bunshaft of Skidmore, Owings & Merrill with Brooks, Barr, Graeber and White, dedicated 1971

Designed and constructed in conjunction with the Lyndon Baines Johnson Library and Museum, this low, 935-foot-long building provides a backdrop to its more monumental neighbor. Speaking of the presidential library, Gordon Bunshaft once commented, "That long building behind it with these different libraries and offices was, as far as we were concerned, a fence to hide the parking behind."

The 275,000-square-foot "fence" has three distinct segments housing the LBJ School of Public Affairs, the Dolph Briscoe Center for American History, and the

Nettie Lee Benson Latin American Collection and the Teresa Lozano Long Institute of Latin American Studies. The upper floors are treated as a gridded concrete volume that sit tenuously on thin concrete columns with dark glass behind and seemingly float above the shadowy void. The horizontal articulation of the building makes its length seem even more extreme.

The sally ports through the building as well as the covered walkway around the perimeter are well suited to the hot Texas climate. Huge sheets of dark bronze glass provide generous visual connection between inside and outside while maintaining protection from the sun. The light well in the center of the main sally port that connects the parking lot with the LBJ Library balances beautifully the contrast between the bright exterior and the dark shaded space within.

The building was named for Sid W. Richardson, a Fort Worth oil producer who had given a two million dollar gift to the university for the purpose of acquiring a renowned collection of libraries of scientific history.

ACKNOWLEDGMENTS

The production of this book would not have been possible without the support of the Office of the President of The University of Texas at Austin. Particular thanks go to President Bill Powers and to Geoffrey Leavenworth who shepherded the process along. We have been inspired by the early and enduring interest in the architecture of the campus by Blake Alexander and Roxanne Williamson and are indebted to Carol McMichael's pioneering work on Paul Cret, Margaret Berry's meticulous compilation of building histories, and the ongoing research and generosity of Jim Nicar. The questions and observations of our students have challenged our thinking and prompted new areas of inquiry. Fortuitously, our work coincided with the study for a historic preservation plan for the Forty Acres led by our colleagues Michael Holleran and Fran Gale. Samuel Dodd paved the way as our first graduate research assistant and was expertly succeeded by Emily Freeman Reed. Graduate students Shannon Halley, Diana Su, and Erin Tyson also contributed. The Page Southerland Page Fellowship in Architecture and the Lawrence W. Speck Excellence Fund provided financial support for research. We are beneficiaries of the knowledge of Beth Dodd, Donna Coates, and Nancy Sparrow at the Alexander Architectural Archive and Margaret Schlankey and her staff at the Dolph Briscoe Center for American History. Eleanor Gillers was our guide at the New-York Historical Society. Sarah Cleary has lent her research skills and sharp eye to all aspects of the project. Among the many UT faculty and staff members who assisted us, we note Paul Bommer who revealed the secrets of the Chemical and Petroleum Engineering Building. Casey Dunn's photographs vividly document the campus today. Dan Simon capably managed the book through production.

INTRODUCTION

1. William J. Battle to UT president T. S. Painter, 13 March 1948. William J. Battle Papers, Box 4P238, Dolph Briscoe Center for American History (CAH).

2. Battle, notes for a history of the construction program at UT, 1925–1935, Battle Papers, Box 4P238, CAH.

3. Paul Cret, "Report Accompanying the General Plan of Development," January 1933, 5. CAH.

4. Battle to Cret, telegram, 8 October 1931; Cret to Battle, 14 October 1932. Battle Papers, 2K245, CAH.

5. Lynn Landrum, "Thinking Out Loud," *The Dallas Morning News*, 26 November, 1949, III-5; quoted in Richard R. Brettell and Willis Cecil Winters, *Crafting Traditions: The Architecture of Mark Lemmon* (Dallas: Meadows Museum and SMU Press, 2005), 74–5.

6. For Erwin's remarks and a concise account of the incident, see Richard A. Holland, "Thirteen Ways of Looking at Chairman Frank," in *The Texas Book*, vol. 1, 60–4.

7. *The Daily Texan*, 15 August 1990.

8. Cesar Pelli & Associates, Balmori Associates, Inc., *University of Texas at Austin Campus Master Plan* (Austin: University of Texas at Austin, 1999).

WALK TWO

1. Quoted by Chloe Lee Quebedeaux, *Housing of Women Students at the University of Texas*, M.A. thesis, University of Texas at Austin, 1938: 26.

SELECTED BIBLIOGRAPHY

A NOTE ON SOURCES

The pioneering texts examining the architectural history of the campus are Williamson (1965), McMichael (1983), and Berry (1993). A valuable forthcoming book is Jim Nicar, *A University for Texas: Essays on the History of the University of Texas*. The monthly magazine of the Texas Exes, *Alcalde*; the student newspaper, *The Daily Texan*; and *Cactus*, the student yearbook, have covered campus buildings throughout their long publication histories. The primary archival collections are housed in the university's Alexander Architectural Archive and the Dolph Briscoe Center for American History, which is the repository for the university's administrative records.

GENERAL

Allen, Kathryn Romona. "A Study of the Evolution of the Philosophy of Student Housing at the University of Texas at Austin from 1883 to 1973," Ph.D. diss., The University of Texas at Austin, 1975.

Battle, William James and H. Y. Benedict. "The Construction Program of the University of Texas, 1925–35," *The American School and University*, vol. 7 (1935), 55–61.

Bay, Deborah Lynn. "The Influence of Frank Erwin on Texas Higher Education," Ph.D. diss., The University of Texas at Austin, 1988.

Benedict, H. Y. *A Source Book Relating to the History of the University of Texas: Legislative, Legal, Bibliographical, and Statistical (University of Texas Bulletin no. 1757)*. Austin: University of Texas, 1917.

Berry, Margaret C. "Student Life and Customs at The University of Texas, 1883–1933," Ed.D. diss., Columbia University, 1965.

_____. *The University of Texas: A Pictorial Account of Its First Century*. Austin: University of Texas Press, 1980.

_____. *Brick by Golden Brick: A History of Campus Buildings at the University of Texas at Austin*. Austin: LBCo. Publishing, 1993.

Brettell, Richard R. and Willis Cecil Winters. *Crafting Traditions: The Architecture of Mark Lemmon*. Dallas: Meadows Museum and SMU Press, 2005.

Brown, Nugent E. *B Hall, Texas: Stories of and about the Famous Dormitory, Brackenridge Hall, Texas University*. San Antonio: The Naylor Company, 1938.

Christen, Barbara Snowden. "Cass Gilbert and the Ideal of the City Beautiful: City and Campus Plans, 1900–1916," Ph.D. diss., City University of New York, 1997.

Cret, Paul. "Report Accompanying the General Plan of Development." Report to the Board of Regents of The University of Texas, January 1933. Austin, TX: 1933.

Dettmer, David. "When the Poor Boys Ruled the Campus: A Requiem for B. Hall," in *The Texas Book: Profiles, History, and Reminiscences of the University*, edited by Richard A. Holland. Austin: University of Texas Press, 2006, 105–124.

Ellison, S. P., Jr. and Joseph J. Jones. *Walking the Forty Acres: Building Stones – Precambrian to Pleistocene*. Austin: The University of Texas at Austin, Retired Faculty-Staff Association, 1984.

Etlin, Richard A. *Symbolic Space: French Enlightenment Architecture and Its Legacy*. Chicago: University of Chicago Press, 1994.

Gribben, Alan. *Harry Huntt Ransom: Intellect in Motion*. Austin: University of Texas Press, 2008.

History of the Residence Halls. The University of Texas at Austin Division of Housing and Food Service. http://www.utexas.edu/student/housing/index.php?site=8&scode=0&is_main=1

Holland, Richard A., ed. *The Texas Book: Profiles, History, and Reminiscences of the University*. Austin: University of Texas Press, 2006.

_____. "Thirteen Ways of Looking at Chairman Frank," in *The Texas Book: Profiles, History, and Reminiscences of the University*, edited by Richard A. Holland, 53–74. Austin: University of Texas Press, 2006.

Jones, Joseph. *Life on Waller Creek: A Palavar about History as Pure and Applied Education*. Austin: AAR/Tantalus, 1982.

McMichael, Carol. *Paul Cret at Texas: Architectural Drawing and the Image of the University in the 1930s*. Exhib. cat. Austin: Archer M. Huntington Art Gallery, The University of Texas at Austin, 1983.

Morse, Frederic C. *The Ex-Student's History of the University of Texas at Austin in Pictures*. Privately printed, 1970.

Speck, Lawrence W. "A Greater Whole." *Texas Architect* 49, no. 1 (January–February 1999): 38–41.

_____. "The University of Texas: Vision and Ambition," in *Cass Gilbert, Life and Work: Architect of the Public Domain*, edited by Barbara S. Christen and Steven Flanders, 192–205. New York: W. W. Norton, 2001.

_____. "Campus Architecture: The Heroic Decades," in *The Texas Book: Profiles, History, and Reminiscences of the University*, edited by Richard A. Holland. Austin: University of Texas Press, 2006, 105–124.

Turner, Paul Venable. *Campus: An American Planning Tradition*. Cambridge, MA: MIT University Press, 1984.

University of Texas at Austin, Cesar Pelli & Associates, and Balmori Associates, Inc. *The University of Texas at Austin Campus Master Plan*. Austin: University of Texas at Austin, 1999.

UT *History Central*. The Texas Exes. http://www.texasexes.org/uthistory/

Williamson, Roxanne Kuter. "A History of the Campus and Buildings of the University of Texas with Emphasis on the Sources for the Architectural Styles," 1965, photocopy.

WALK ONE

Bobb, F. Scott. "Texas Union Reopens," *Alcalde* 65, no. 1 (September/October 1977): 26–31.

Connolly, Lawrence. "A Monolith Clearly Redefined Harry Ransom Center." *Texas Architect* 54 no. 2 (March-April 2004): 30–33.

Dillon, David. "Best Laid Plans," [review of Goldsmith Hall addition and renovation] *Architecture* 79 (November 1989): 84–89.

"Doctor, Lawyer, Merchant, Chief: There's Something for Everyone in the Automated, Computerized College Where Innovation is the Incentive," [Business Administration – Economics Building] *Alcalde* 57, no. 6 (February 1969): 10–13.

Harris, August Watkins. "Cass Gilbert's Old Library Building: The Eugene C. Barker Texas History Center, 1910-1960," *Southwestern Historical Quarterly* 64 (July 1960): 1–12.

"Library of University of Texas, Austin, Texas, Cass Gilbert, Architect." *Architecture* 26 (15 December 1912): 110–113.

Ochsner, Jeffrey Karl. "The Renewal of Sutton Hall: Architecture Complex Taking Shape at UT-Austin." *Texas Architect* 33, no. 2 (March-April 1983): 60–63.

Rolfe, Walter T. "Architecture." *Alcalde* (December 1933): 55–6, 61.

Wagnon, Susan Elizabeth. "A History of the Texas Union at the University of Texas at Austin," M.A. thesis, The University of Texas at Austin, 1971.

WALK TWO

Duren, Almetris Marsh with Louise Iscoe. *Overcoming a History of Black Integration at the University of Texas at Austin.* Austin: University of Texas at Austin, 1979.

Quebedeaux, Chloe Lee. "Housing of Women Students at The University of Texas," M.A. thesis, The University of Texas at Austin, 1938.

WALK THREE

Andersson, Arthur. "Psychology Today." *Texas Architect* 53, no. 4 (July–August 2003): 34-37.

McCaslin, Richard B. and Dean Earnest F. Gloyna. *Commitment to Excellence: One Hundred Years of Engineering Education at The University of Texas at Austin.* Austin: The Engineering Foundation of the College of Engineering, The University of Texas at Austin, 1986.

Vernooy, Andrew D., and Kevin Alter. "Hi-tech Unrevealed UT ACES Building, Austin." *Texas Architect* 51, no. 1 (January–February 2001): 28–31.

WALK FOUR

Gunderson, W. Mark. "A Flaw in the System: A Battle over Architecture Strips the University of Texas of a Signature Building, *Cite: The Architecture and Design Review of Houston* 47 (Spring 2000): 34–37.

Brettell, Richard R. "A Question of Size: The Blanton Museum Gives Austin a Notable Art Collection, but a Less Notable Building to House It." *Cite: The Architecture and Design Review of Houston* 69 (Winter 2006): 14–17.

Oberholzer, Mark. "The Art of Deference: Jack S. Blanton Museum of Art, Phase I & II, Austin." *Texas Architect* 59, no. 3 (May–June 2009): 56–61.

Tilley, Ray Don. 1991. "Alumni Cheer: Doc and Gertrude Neuhaus Expansion, Lila B. Etter Alumni Center, University of Texas at Austin." *Architecture: The AIA Journal* 80, no. 3 (March 1991): 70–73.

WALK FIVE

Pennington, Richard. *"For Texas, I Will:" The History of Memorial Stadium.* Austin: Historical Publications, 1992.

Tillotson, Steven Land. *Remnant of an Era: The History of the Little Campus Site, (1859-1977).* Austin, TX: University of Texas School of Architecture, 1977.

WALK SIX

Connolly, Lawrence. "Second Act Bass Concert Hall Renovation and Expansion, Austin." *Texas Architect* 60, no. 2 (March–April 2010): 52–55.

——— "Gordon Bunshaft (1909–1990)." Transcript of interview conducted by Betty J. Blum, 1989. Chicago Architects Oral History Project, Art Institute of Chicago.

Huxtable, Ada Louise. "A Success as Architecture and Monument," *The New York Times* (May 23, 1971): 39.

Krinsky, Carol Herselle. *Gordon Bunshaft of Skidmore, Owings & Merrill.* Cambridge, MA: MIT Press, 1988.

All photography by Casey Dunn, © Princeton Architectural Press unless otherwise noted.

[Fig 1] Page 11: PICA 22984, Austin History Center, Austin Public Library

[Fig 2] Page 12: Prints and Photographs Collection, The Dolph Briscoe Center for American History, The University of Texas at Austin

[Fig 3] Page 13: Prints and Photographs Collection, The Dolph Briscoe Center for American History, The University of Texas at Austin, CN11285

[Fig 4] Page 14: Credit: Prints and Photographs Collection, The Dolph Briscoe Center for American History, The University of Texas at Austin

[Fig 5] Page 15: Prints and Photographs Collection, The Dolph Briscoe Center for American History, The University of Texas at Austin

[Fig 6] Page 18–19: New-York Historical Society

[Fig 7] Page 21: Prints and Photographs Collection, The Dolph Briscoe Center for American History, The University of Texas at Austin

[Fig 8] Page 24: University of Texas – Office of the President, Vf15 D.b, The Dolph Briscoe Center for American History, The University of Texas at Austin, CN 09947

[Fig 9] Page 26: Prints and Photographs Collection, The Dolph Briscoe Center for American History, The University of Texas at Austin, di 04251.

[Fig 10] Page 29: Paul Philippe Cret Collection, Alexander Architectural Archive, The University of Texas at Austin

[Fig 11] Page 30: Paul Philippe Cret Collection, Alexander Architectural Archive, The University of Texas at Austin

[Fig 12] Page 33: Alexander Architectural Archive, The University of Texas at Austin

[Fig 13] Page 34–35: Prints and Photographs Collection, The Dolph Briscoe Center for American History, The University of Texas at Austin

[Fig 14] Page 40: Prints and Photographs Collection, The Dolph Briscoe Center for American History, The University of Texas at Austin

[Fig 15] Page 44: The University of Texas at Austin

[Fig 16] Page 46: Prints and Photographs Collection, The Dolph Briscoe Center for American History, The University of Texas at Austin

[Fig 17] Page 46: Prints and Photographs Collection, The Dolph Briscoe Center for American History, The University of Texas at Austin

INDEX